Race, Regret, and the Reassurance of Love

By

David Matteo

Dedication

To the chosen.

Contents

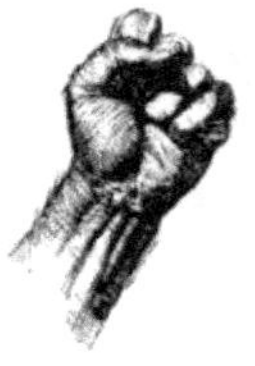

Poems about RACE...............................

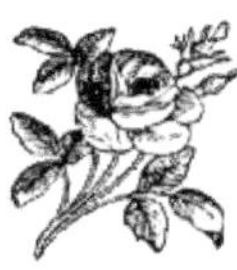

Poems about REGRET.............................

Poems about THE REASSURANCE OF LOVE....

Introduction

The word 'unprecedented'—will forever be synonymous in my mind with the year 2020, and rightfully so, as what we experienced and witnessed may never be felt or seen like this again in our lifetime. It was certainly a year of clarity and exposure, among other things, defined by a deadly plague with a magnitude not seen since biblical times, and make no mistake— we are currently in the midst of those times— and whether you agree or not, I believe the judgement upon this land, and the world, stems from the persecution and systems of oppression placed upon God's chosen people (the 12 Tribes of Israel) over the last 400 years; be it racial, economical, educational or judicial; the Most High is now redeeming his people and directing his anger towards those who were confederate against them. (Reference Genesis 15: 13-14, Deuteronomy 28: 15-68, and Psalms 83.) Although many have placed their hope in science and a vaccine to get us back to "normal", those days, as the world remembers them, are never coming back. I believe the only way for Jews and gentiles to obtain mercy and covering during this time is to acknowledge the Most High (Yahawah) as the true and living God, uncover your heart, repent of your sins, and to bless his chosen people.

In a year full of racial unrest and misinformation, job loss, poverty and mass killings; the silver lining, if you can call it that, was the sense of urgency I felt to accomplish all that I could, knowing that time wasn't a commodity I could afford to waste anymore. Time—was the inspiration and theme behind this collection. Being conscious of where we are in time, I wanted to capture my thoughts and feelings surrounding the series of unprecedented events that unfolded since March 2020 when judgement began— mainly being frustration, anger and regret but above them all, gratitude. The ability to wake up every single day, not by my own will, has reinforced how precious life is especially when thousands of people continue to die each day.

So, if you're reading this, I pray you consider yourself highly blessed, with purpose, because unlike millions of people worldwide, you are still here; we are still here, still counted among the living! And for this gift, I give all praises and honor to the Most High for granting me the time to live and complete this work; the time to strengthen existing relationships and re-connect with those that were lost, time to still love and embrace my family and friends while they yet live, and most of all, the time to grow in knowledge and understanding. He has extended more mercy to me than I deserve in this life, and I'm profoundly grateful for each second of peace because, there is no respect of person with God, and I know that at any moment, my life can be met with certain tragedy and misfortune, regardless of my good works or kind heart—such things do not absolve or exclude me from the wrath of His judgement, being guilty myself of sin every day.

With sincerity, I pray these poems can be used as a source of awareness to shed light on racial injustice, to provide a smile or a laugh, or to inspire positive change in any area of your life that needs it (Trust me, some of these poems were the tough conversations I had to have with myself lol!). My hope is that you continue to make the best use of your time while you're still here because life truly is uncertain, with no guarantees. To quote the book of Sirach, Chapter 51:30- "Work your work before the time comes, and in his time he will give you your reward."

Lastly, with all your strength, love the one who created you and love yourself completely.

Peace.

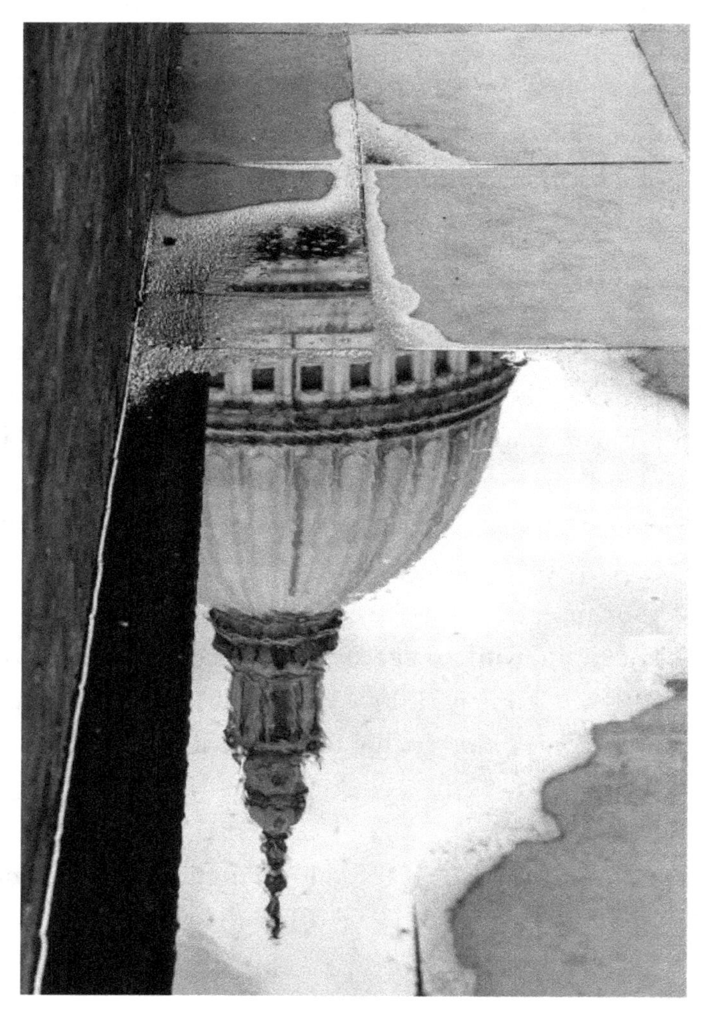

The Audacity

*Ain't this a b*tch!*
You know—actually being arrested and convicted for
the heinous crimes you commit?
Especially when you foolishly record the offense that
reveals your identity?
Since when??
Since when is it illegal to storm federal grounds in an
organized attack,
Damaging and stealing property at the Nation's
Capitol,
Galvanizing others to violence because the majority of
the country chose a Democrat?
Aren't you well within your rights to protest such a
tragedy, being an extreme faction?
Of course you are!
Because how dare we tell you how to act in YOUR
house!
The lack of excessive force when YOU break the
rules, further highlights the inequalities and racial disparities
experienced by minorities in this country because we all know,
for a surety,
That had those faces been black, the police would not
have acted so graciously towards US.
And the results, unequivocally,
Would have been drastically different—
Period.

*But I bet you wish you could retract your statements
and actions now though, huh?
Now that white nationalists are demonized and
deemed the greatest threat to this country;
That's funny…
Seems like you've lost your protection in the execution
of your deadly siege, with authorities still finding you in your
failed, sneaky retreat;
But thankfully there's nowhere to hide and no more
disguises!
You've been identified in plain sight, exposed for the
world to see, and I assure you this story won't be misconstrued
as "fake news";
What we saw is EXACTLY who you are and who
you've always been—
And I guarantee history won't confuse your
"heroism" for "patriotism" again after this;
Not this time.*

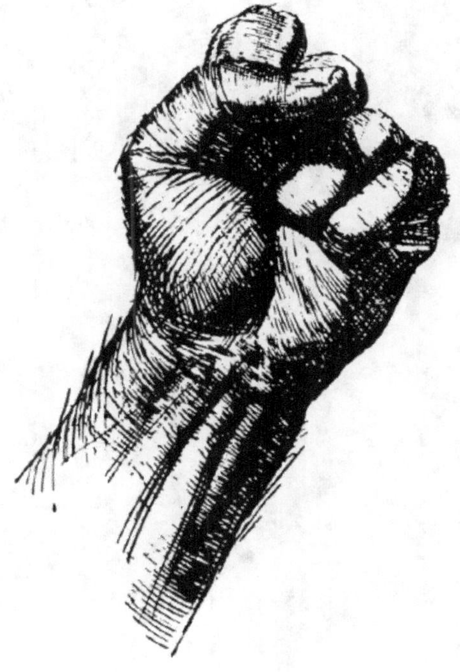

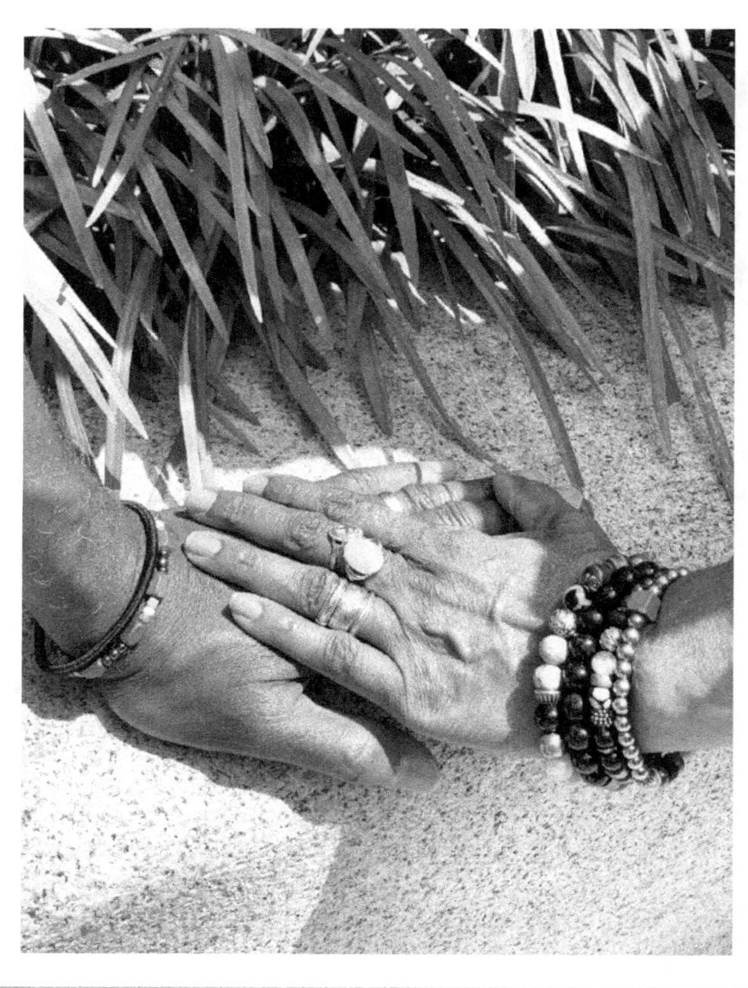

Even After

Beloved,
Even until my dying breath,
No force on Earth will ever make me forget that
alluring moment we met,
Nor the second our eyes connected for the first time;
With your hand in mine walking under heaven's
ocean;
Brilliant rays of sun, shining brightly in its highest
ascension,
Ignited a desire so intense,
That past, future and present tense all existed in an
instant, from a simple stroke of summer heat;
My face flushed, laden with anxiety, anticipating the
touch of your forward advance;
My heart trapped in a whirl of wanderlust,
Blissfully swimming through your field of paradise,
where flowers dance in the wind and birds sail the open skies;
Free—
In a place with no end or beginning, where my only
escape was through your lips;
And now my own, finally being granted permission
to roam,
Dared to discover the secrets behind your kiss,
Which found me and took me hostage to a state of
sweet delirium;
And from that moment, I became a fugitive no longer

on the run, Neither one afraid to be captured under
love's dominion but willingly succumbed;
To you only did I submit,
The greatest gift anyone can ever receive in the
pursuit of true love,
And it remains yours, and forever will be,
Even after.

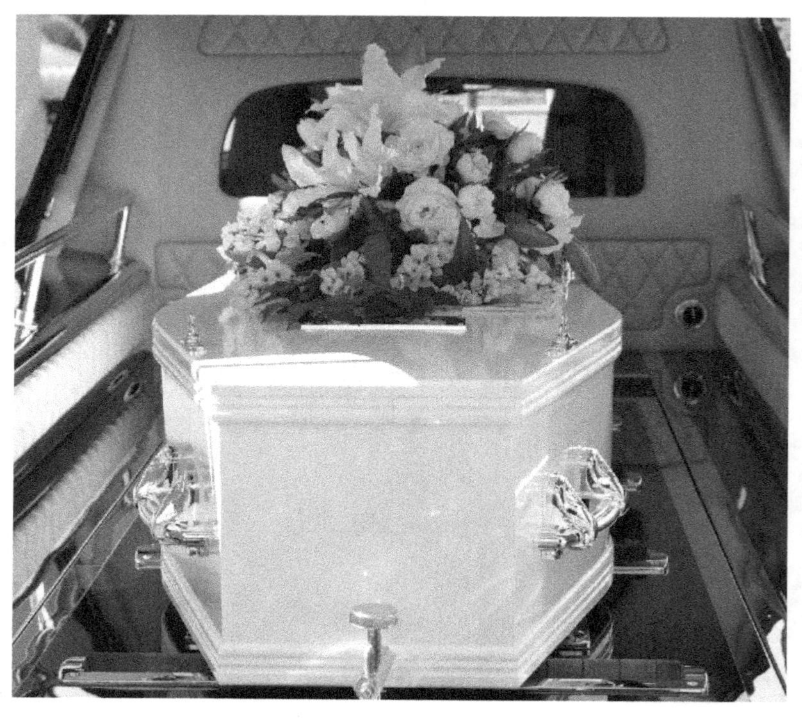

Good Grief

*Standing above you, viewing your face for the last
time,
I shed my final tears considering the state of my own
mortality;
Reminded that this life is temporary, with an
uncertain destination that inevitably awaits us all too soon;
Initially, a select few honored your memory with
amusing anecdotes and profound words;
Stating our breath is a gift from God that's revoked
upon death; a debt repaid for our lease to live,
Which didn't fall mute on attentive ears, but that
insight was blighted from the spectacle that followed;
The one woman show who stole the glory of your
legacy;
Who boldly stood before the family with the audacity
to label us miscreants guilty of malfeasance;
Proudly professing to possess holiness yet vigorously,
Defiled your name and profession with a performance
so unsettling it'll never be forgiven,
Nor forgotten for its rotten and disgraceful delivery.
It's abundantly clear she covets the diadem of
matriarch you once held but she'll never be accepted;
Her white robe has been stained crimson—
Drenched with vanity and deceit, that we need not
worry about seeking vengeance;
For in due time, she'll receive the reward for her*

misdeeds and be made to pay;
You already know what they say about karma, so I'll
save the expletive out of respect;
Especially for the misappropriation of funds that
was never collected by your intended recipients—
But I digress…
The word of truth, which you impressed upon us, is
what we'll continue to stand on until the very end;
And come hell or high water, we'll always defend the
beauty of your prestige,
Never letting your teachings or branch be severed from
the body of this family,
Not even by our own.

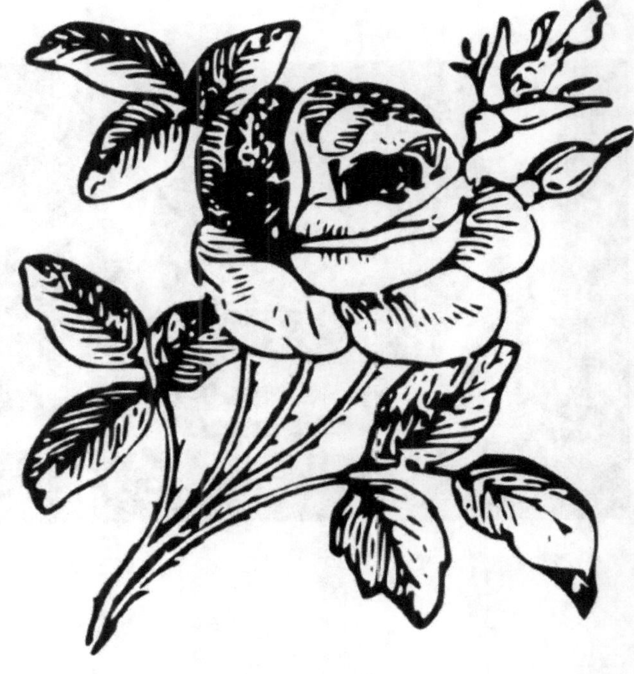

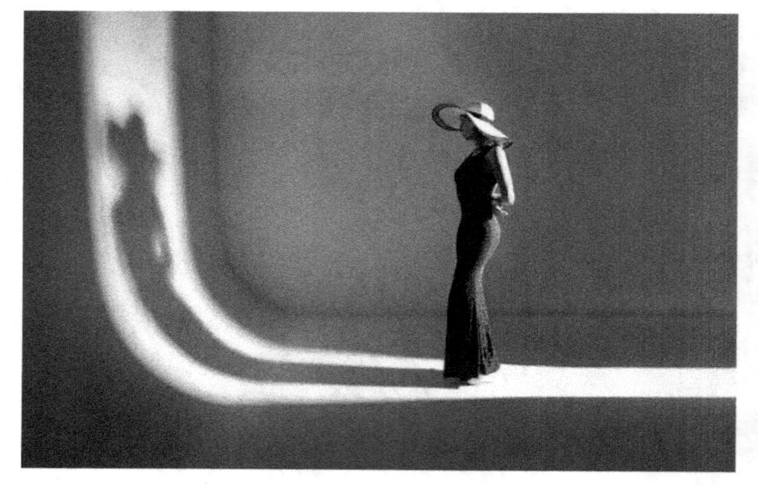

Dear Stranger

*I imagine it's been quite some time since my last
message;
Forgive me,
As I didn't want to seem too selfish or demanding in
my entreaties;
I respect your space and understand you have
competing priorities, so I'll be brief;
Prayerfully this letter reaches you at the correct
address,
Because the details contained within, are by far the
most sincere arrangement of words I think I've ever
assembled;
Humbly, I request your full attention and
consideration of this desperate plea;
Let this serve as notice,
That I won't stand by idly, and allow your absence
to disturb my tranquility for another second;
Most of my days are spent searching for you
relentlessly, but sadly to no avail;
And although your appearance be unknown to me,
And the mysteries of your soul have not been made
privy,
Somehow, every minute, I envision being held in your
loving arms, with your embrace bringing peace to my troubled
mind;
My head laying upon your shoulder, finding rest from*

the mental distress that weighs so heavily;
And my spirit comforted, in the security your eyes
convey when they look at me, that I have nothing to fear.
How long must this drought of loneliness continue
until you spring forth and appear?
I shudder to think,
But your presence is needed now more than you could
ever know;
I beg you to make this dream a reality and reveal
your identity whoever you are, wherever you are;
Please—
Find your way to me, by any means necessary, and
bring,
Love.

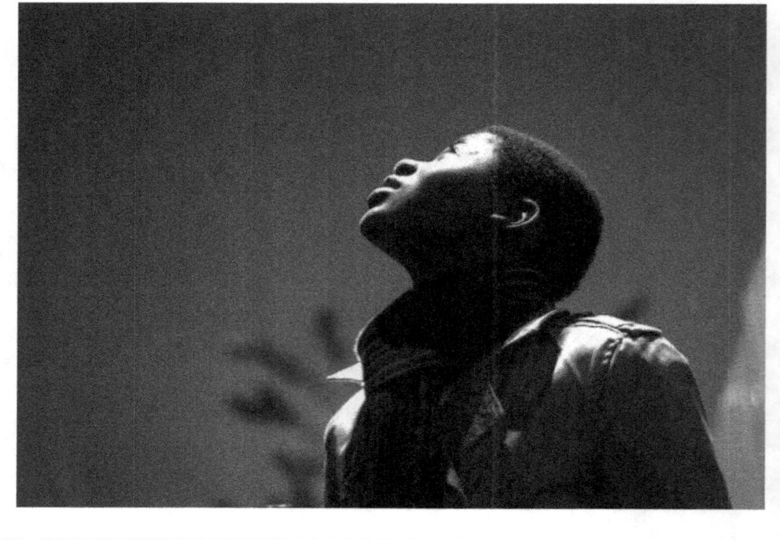

Election Integrity

*After so many years, my mind still can't seem to
fathom;*
*That from every descendant in my past, who
survived all manner of inconceivable torture, you chose me, to
be among the living now;*
*I consider it an honor and privilege to be present at
such a time as this, but just out of curiosity, which qualities
of mine actually won your vote?*
It would truly help me to know,
*For I find that in my moments of sorrow, it's the
mystery of your selection that gives me hope;*
*When I meditate on the words spoken in Jeremiah
1:5,*
*I can't help but ascribe them as a personalized note to
me;*
*A sacred promise and assurance that you knew me
before I was formed;*
*So after being born, you knew the person I'd turn out
to be;*
*That—is consolation in itself but occasionally, I
tend to wonder if another would have been better suited to live
my life;*
*One who would've done something greater with the
opportunities and favor you afforded me;*
Taking advantage of all the advances to progress to

prominence instead of lacking ambition and sulking
in obscurity;
Is it wrong to feel like a mistake?
Because at times, I honestly don't see the value in the
space I occupy,
But don't get me wrong—
By no means do I wish to dissuade your interest in
bestowing grace,
Nor do I intend to question your omniscience, but,
To finally end this internal debate;
In my last attempt for seeking validation,
Tell me—
Was I really the best candidate?

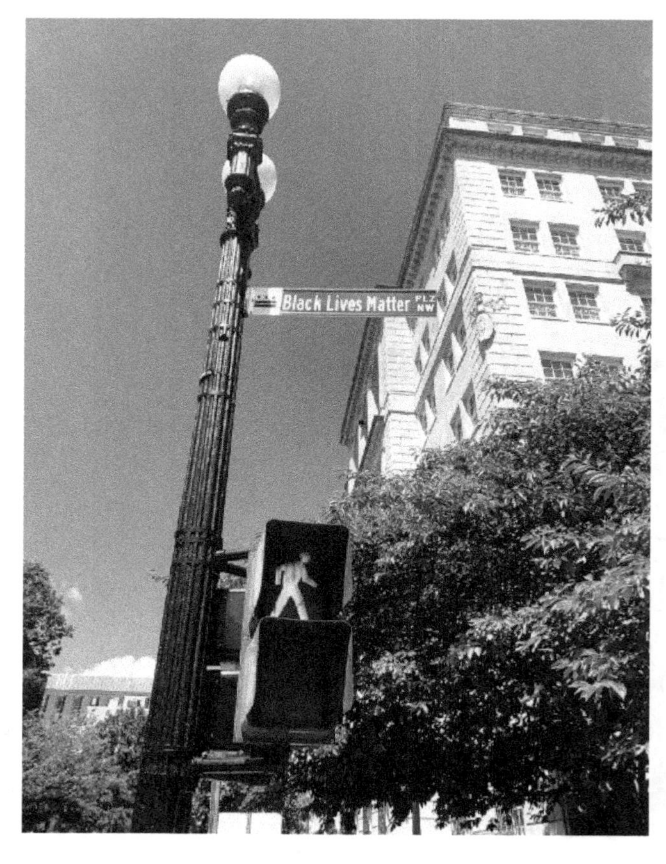
Black Lives Matter PLZ NW

Had Enough?

*There's nothing more to say that hasn't already been
said;
Neither anything further to do to persuade
disbelievers;
The painful truth is that our continued fight for
democracy we seem to labor in vain——
Policed by those who swear by the law of liberty, but
deign to uphold that very oath;
Is it me?
Or does the promise of freedom quickly fade with
each slain body laid to rest,
Followed by a hashtag with "best wishes" and
"thoughts and prayers" for the oppressed——
Then constantly being asked to forgive these racists
for the same mistakes,
Time and time again,
Without repercussion,
Is f*cking exhausting and I'm tired of them
pretending prejudice doesn't exist!
Skip the "let's have a conversation" bullsh*t, because
you genuinely have no interest in saving lives but only
spreading lies, even during a pandemic!
Where thousands of people have died through
deliberate negligence, seemingly at our leaders behest!
What a travesty when our tragedies are mourned less*

especially by those we elect;
Our country being viciously ravaged by death via an
"unknown" threat,
Was sadly only "unknown" to the people most
affected…
Still, their egregious deceit is the ultimate sign of
disrespect;
Their blatant disregard for our intellect stripped us
the ability to protect ourselves, and now what do we have left?
Confusion and discord quickly spreading to every
corner of the globe;
Until the trusted are discredited and the liars being
faithfully adored;
Well, I for one can no longer afford to place my faith
in a system that profits me nothing;
Haven't I paid enough?
Haven't WE paid enough?

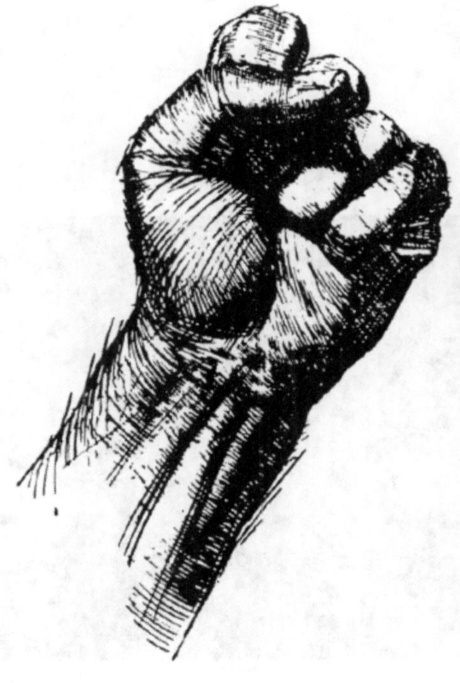

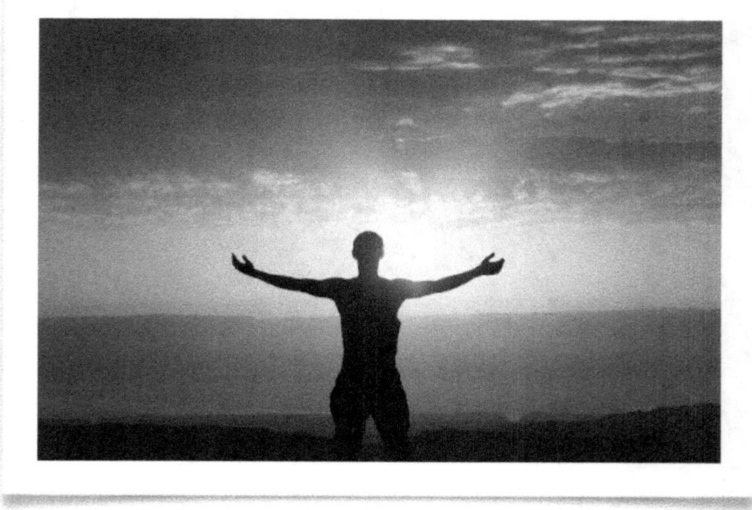

Self-absorbed

I can't believe I was really that delusional back then;
Why didn't anybody tell me about this sooner!
Thank God for YouTube or I'd still be clueless about
this truly revolutionary discovery!
Now granted—
Sex and the desire to cum, was all that preoccupied
my pubescent mind in high school,
But had someone told me about the benefits of semen
retention, I definitely wouldn't have been so reckless in my
tireless crusade;
Hopefully, this topic is incorporated in sex education
today because I, for one, feel betrayed;
That this information was never disclosed or
conveyed in a way that genuinely stressed the importance;
This substance, literally being the life energy that
fuels our masculinity:
Improves self-esteem, promotes better sleep and a
stronger motivation to succeed;
Provides increased immunity, brain clarity and
enhanced creativity;
Supports muscle growth, sharper focus and better
sexual performance;
Apparently the list goes on and on when you don't get
off!
And there's absolutely no substitute for the power of

manifestation you can channel through transmutation

—

Nothing at all!
But still don't believe me and need proof?
Try it for yourself and see how you feel; I guarantee
that after the first week, you'll definitely notice a change!
My life surely did, after I decided to safeguard my
most sacred treasure;
Reinforcing what I knew must be protected at all
costs—
My future!
So don't let yours slip down the drain either!
A friendly piece of advice you can have for free;
You're welcome!

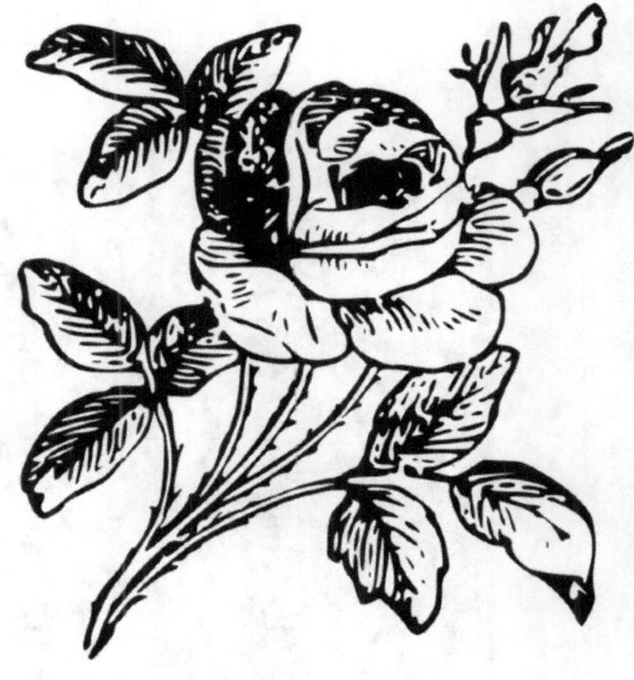

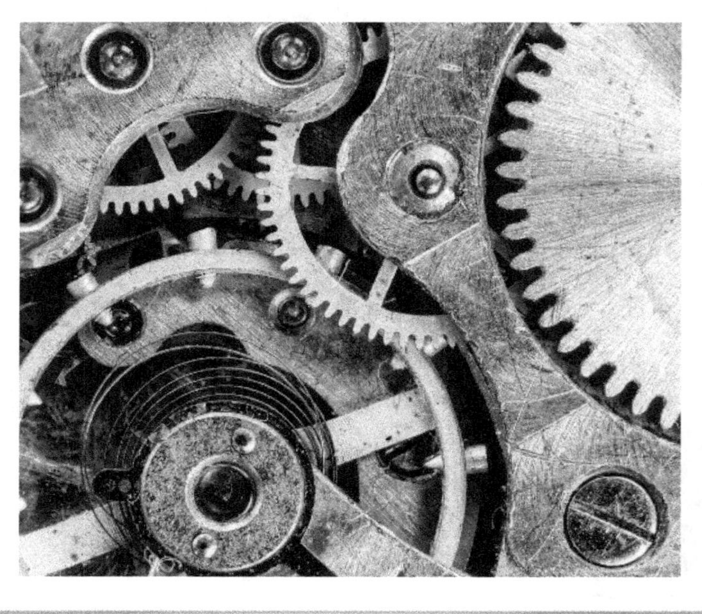

Switch Gears

At long last!!!
After being in captivity 4 centuries, our prison
sentence is finally complete!
The holy covenant of Abraham has been restored,
and our divine shift has been set in motion!
The remnant who remains are lucky to be counted
among the chosen,
As the beneficiaries of salvation for which our
ancestors lamented;
What a glorious sight it will be!
To behold your majesty and the beautiful wrath of
your promise foretold long ago,
That all your children slain, shall be avenged on that
great and terrible day;
With thousands falling on every side, only with our
eyes shall we witness the reward of the wicked—
And it has begun!
As we witnessed the Great Conjunction of our three
largest stars,
All resting at zero in space herald the Great Reset!
Ending the era of oppression on the first day of the
new solstice;
Signifying that time is winding down for the other
nations, and their hold on us is broken;

Winter is coming indeed!
With sweet retribution being served by fire this time
around!
And I know the angels and spirits rejoice, with
heavenly countenance for the age that follows,
Because we'll never be enslaved again!
Encumbered by chains will not define or identify us
henceforth; we are enlightened and free!
And shall live beside our Mighty King, in perfect
harmony, free from sin,
Forevermore!

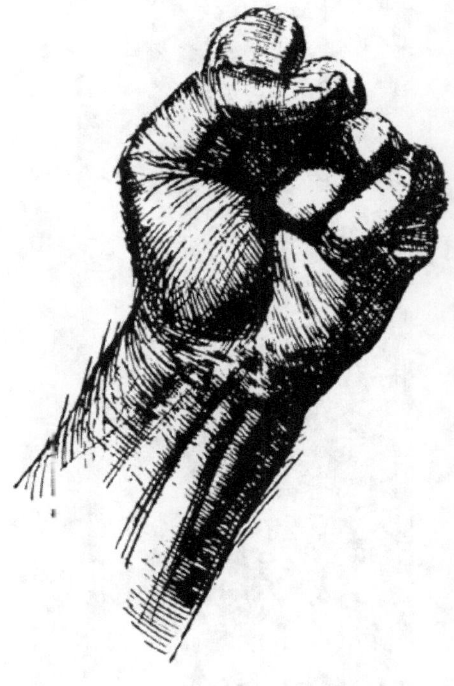

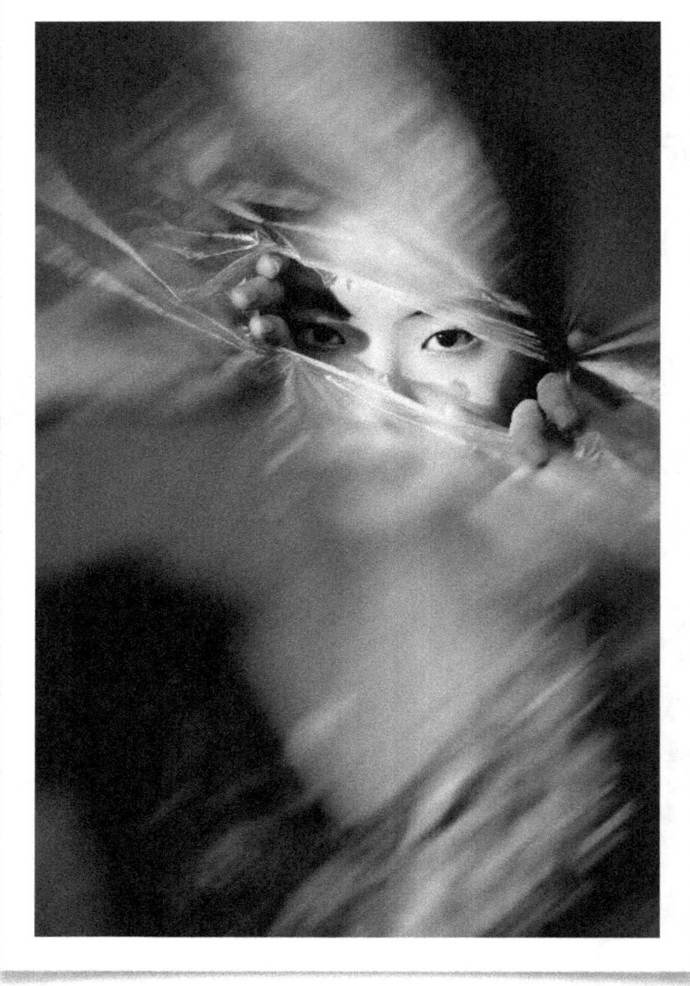

Peekaboo

I know you've been use to the usual tactic of
deflection—
But the "invisible enemy" can actually be seen if you
know where to look;
He's been right in front of you all along!
But don't be fooled by his disappearing act because
as you can see, this plague isn't going anywhere;
WHO do I think is really to blame, might you ask?
Let me refresh your memory of the past, lest we
forget;
The man who stood in front of the press and advised
us all to ingest disinfectant;
The one who conspired with, and encouraged foreign
interference to guarantee his re-election;
The man who ignored sound advice, shipping vital
supplies to other countries needed domestically,
To combat a deadly virus he knew the severity of, but
denied its existence;
The one who refused to condemn violence from white
nationalists, encouraging these racists to liberate their states;
The same man who pardoned criminals while being
guilty himself of fraud and sexual assault, nepotism and
misogyny;
Who desperately stood ready to sacrifice American

lives to stimulate the failing economy—
The man who constructed facilities to separate
families at the border, where hundreds of children have yet to
be reunited,
The one who persecuted immigrant lives seeking
asylum; habitually unsympathetic for his divisive rhetoric;
concerned only with matters that benefit a certain race and
class,
I ask—
Is the agenda not evident to you yet?
That your death seems to be of no consequence in
comparison to dollars and cents!
Doesn't it bother you, that the value of your life was
waged without your knowledge or consent?
I don't know about you, but it's pretty clear to me;
That none can be trusted within this governing body
that loves to create barriers through division—
And as tall as your wall is, there's no way you can
ever hide your cruel intentions;
Surprise, surprise!
I still see you!

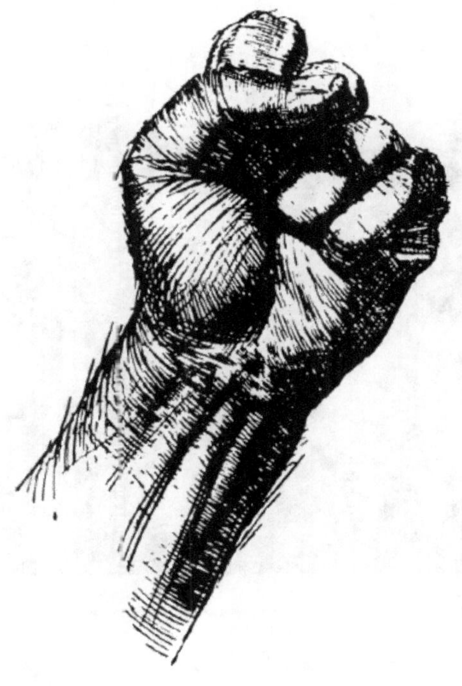

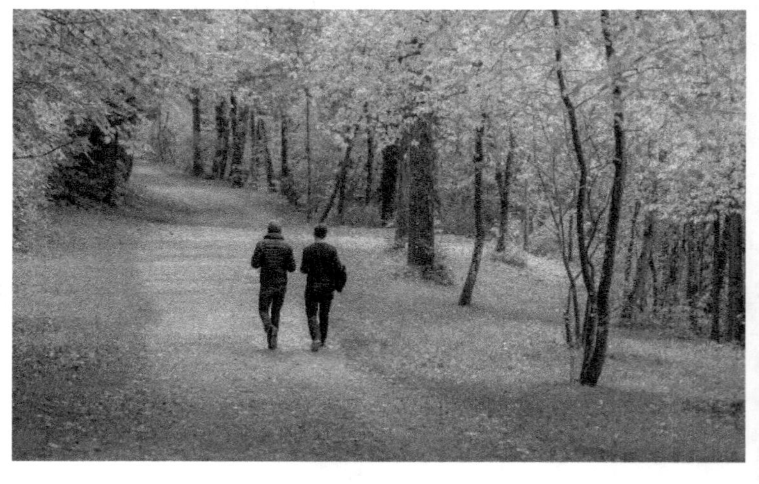

Pep Talk

STOP!
NOT. ANOTHER. WORD.
You don't deserve to complain and frankly, I'm sick
*of your bullsh*t;*
Don't fix your lips to utter more absurdity to gain my
sympathy because I'm not interested, in the least—
You consult me for my input but never follow my
advice,
So why should I NOW listen to you cry about your
life's regrets and lack of direction?
Here's a tip—
*GROW. THE. F*CK. UP. and TAKE.*
ACCOUNTABILITY!!!
We both know you're fully capable of producing
more than you are currently, but you're lazy!
Oh, you mad???
Well good!
I hate to unleash this diatribe against your delicate
pride but, did I lie?
I refuse to accept any more excuses because for God's
sake, you're not even trying!
You've been fully apprised of the sacrifices it takes,
So for your lack of effort, I surmise you're content in
your descent, and won't continue to pacify your inaction!

Now— because I love you, Imma tell you this one
last time…and hear me well—
You have everything you need to get everything you
want;
The only thing truly standing in your way IS YOU!
So quell the fear you harbor, and transform that
negative energy to propel you to destiny,
YOU CAN DO THIS!
Now,
Get to work!

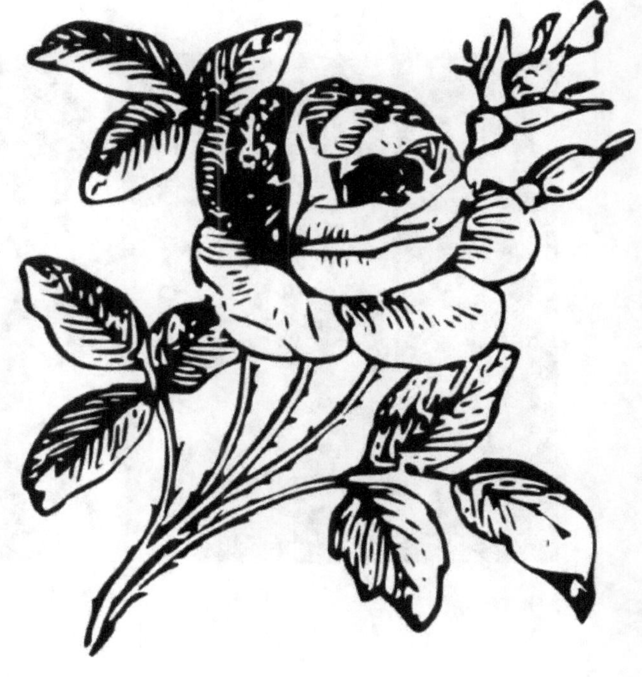

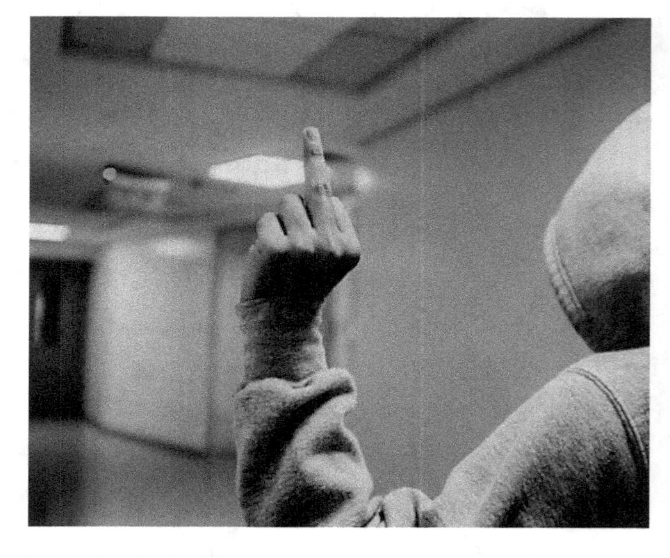

U&IR1

You know what,
*Miss me with that lovey-dovey sh*t because if that*
was the case,
Why was our relationship not fixed?
Why did you deliberately violate my trust, and
deviate from the commitment we both agreed to uphold?
Together!
Or don't you remember you promised me forever?
Those pleasant words combined, I find,
Were only used to placate my frustration from your
incessant lies;
And although you claimed to love me, I was
continuously met with disrespect;
Those two aspects are mutually exclusive and
represent a cause I refuse to advocate for;
Not anymore,
And therefore, have no interest in the preservation of
our union.

Now, in the future, when you assess the details
regarding this separation,
Let it not be mistaken who's to blame;
And as we depart, allow me to leave you with this
little abbreviation, sincerely from the heart—
F.U!

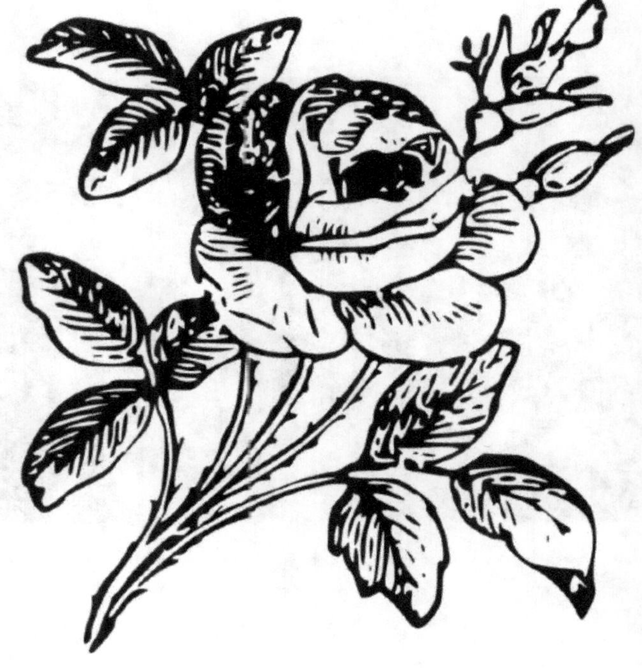

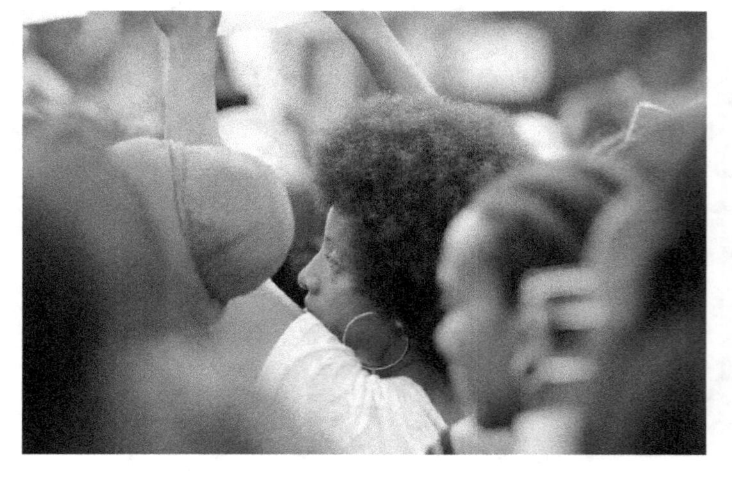

The Great March

Suffice it to say, I've never met a person quite as
exceptional as you;
Extraordinary in fact,
For the successful conquest of your trial by combat
which nearly cost you your life;
A testament to the arduous fight you endured through
the great unknown;
A dangerous journey traveled to a destination with
only one single goal in mind,
Survival!
Your bravery in this tour of duty, even in the face of
great uncertainty, is to be highly commended,
Especially when your brethren suffered a different fate
by way of natural selection;
But against all odds, YOU prevailed!
Overcoming the valiant struggle to pierce that
impenetrable barrier, and all it took was a fracture for you to
break through;
Don't you see?
You're so much stronger than you realize!
If you ever have doubts about your capability in this
life, let that battle serve as a reminder of where your power
lies;
It resides within you!

The windows of heaven are open and doors of defeat
are closed, because you've been chosen!
Remember that millions of your fellow soldiers didn't
make it—
But can you imagine though, who you'd be, if
another one did?
So I salute you Divine Being, and call you victorious
for enduring to the end;
Being among so many until there were only few,
You undoubtedly became,
The one.

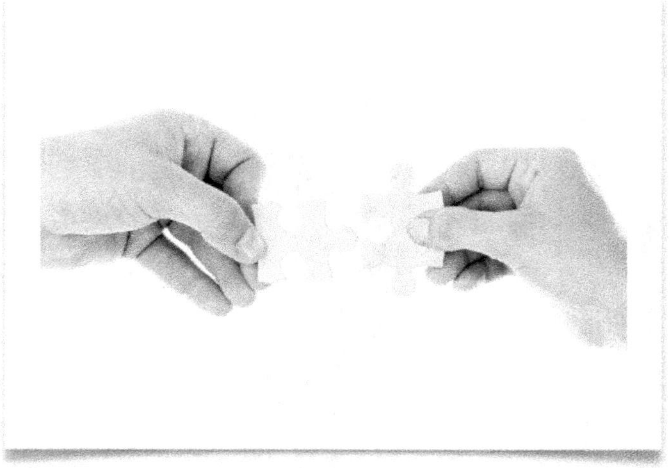

My Apology

I may never get the chance to say this to you in person

—

So in lieu of the plight of our current circumstance,
allow my pen to express the words I've concealed for far too
long;
I utterly despise myself for keeping our love a secret;
I was a coward—
For not having the courage to stand by your side, and
choosing to still live a lie, was my most solemn and deepest
regret;
The one decision I wish I could retract in retrospect,
Because past lovers all pale in comparison to the
special way you made me feel;
The strongest attraction I've ever known;
Which revived my hope and saved my life from the
very first kiss;
And every one that followed I relished deeply, every
kiss, including the last.
Now this may sound daft, I know,
But before you even approached with your bold
introduction, your body told a story;
That concluded with my tool swollen and ready, at
the drop of a dime, to give you this work, early!
That type of chemistry was never present with
anyone else before,

So I knew there was something about you I couldn't

afford to miss—

And I'd be totally remiss not to admit my devastation

that it ended so quickly,

So—

Here I am, missing you,

That even to this day, your scent I still remember,

and your face my mind won't let me forget;

The way your eyes invaded my territory and bested

my fears, laying them all to rest in a sweet surrender was

aggressive yet tender,

Rendering me helpless;

And now, I'm hopeless,

Desperately searching for a replacement who will love

me the way you did;

But I know deep in my heart, there never will be…

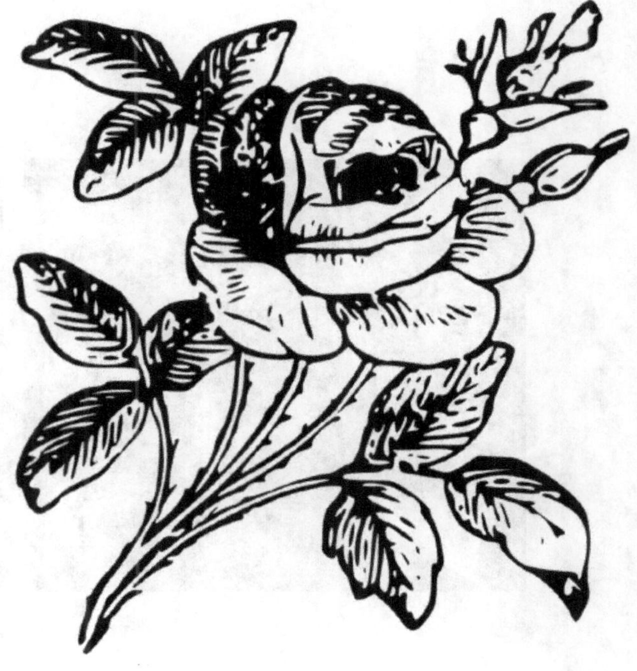

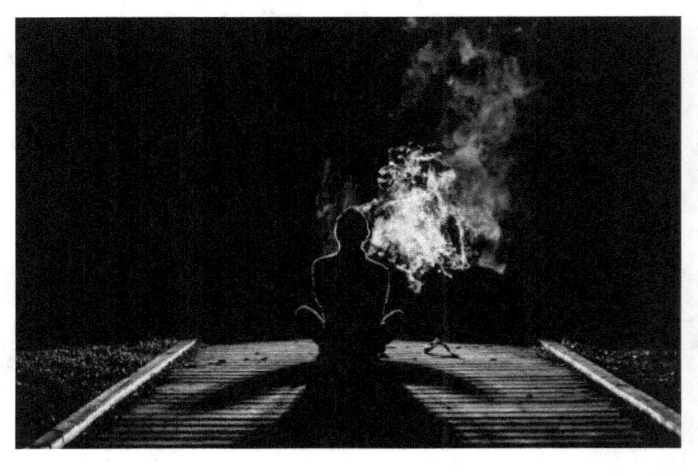

The Drop-off

It's odd for me to admit this but I have a confession;
A random taste to heavily medicate has fostered its
way into my mind,
But don't lambaste me—
The desire for said substance is unfamiliar, yet
strangely, not unwelcome;
Not surprising as I've been expecting its arrival for
quite some time;
An inherent impulse to consume another poison than
my preference presently;
Something slightly more dangerous,
Feeding the itch towards this natural proclivity to
misbehave and elevate;
Don't laugh, but I'm a true reprobate in disguise—
with solid experience under my belt now so I'm ready for the
next level!
A promotion to upper tier with exponential potential
because as I've grown, so has my hunger,
That can no longer be sedated with a tenuous spirit
or narcotic;
I wanna go higher—
High above where the depth of despondency can't
reach my joy;
Because I swear Imma lose it over this nation and
the lack of safety for my people;

Where every day, my heart races and my head
literally aches, dreading the moment another life is taken;
The hope of equality seems to become less of a
reality because in actuality, no one actually cares…
And neither do I at this point,
Not anymore…
So what you bring me?

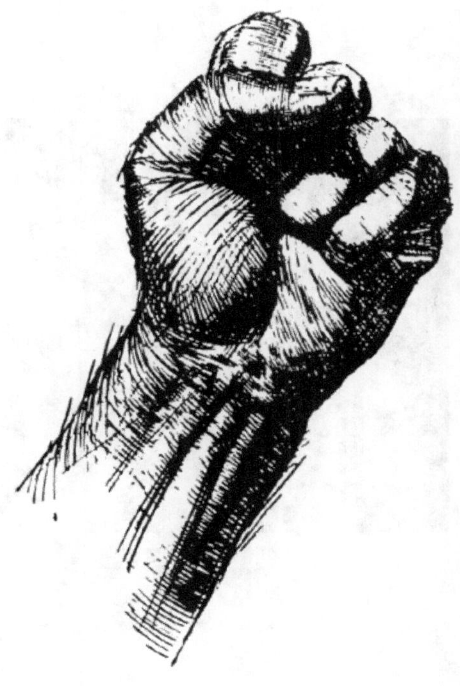

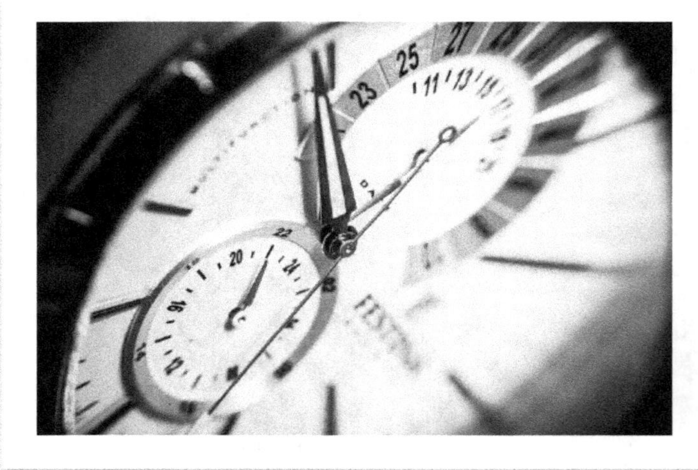

Real Quick

Hey,
Bear with me a sec as I travel this trip down memory
lane;
The subject may be inappropriate in nature, but I
promise it'll be quick—
I just remembered running into an old friend I hadn't
seen in ages;
My namesake, who I met in my early days, cleaning
ships for a living;
We lost contact when my tenure ended and
eventually, he faded from memory,
But as fate would have it,
We re-connected out of state, randomly, at an
amusement park buying drinks at the bar.
Now honestly from the time we became friends, I
never saw him the way I did this day;
And I wondered if he ever felt the same way about
me in the past—
But not surprising, he looked exactly the same, even
younger actually;
So we casually greeted, exchanged numbers and
agreed to meet later that evening to catch up.
Now—for context, I ain't goin lie—the entire
interaction was hella flirtatious, and our conversation revealed

to him, for the first time, what we both shared in
common;
Excitement quickly grew to anxiety though, thinking
about exposure and my experience because,
I'd just got comfortable identifying, and had no prior
encounters to validate me,
And from the intense look in his eyes, I knew exactly
what was on his mind…
So I got scared—and ignored the subsequent
messages he sent;
*A true b*tch move on my end…and subsequently, we*
haven't spoken since;
Another missed opportunity I found a clever way to
circumvent.
Driving home the next day, I was pissed,
disappointed with regret that I let it happen, AGAIN!
DAMMIT!!!
Ugh…
Yeah…
That's it.

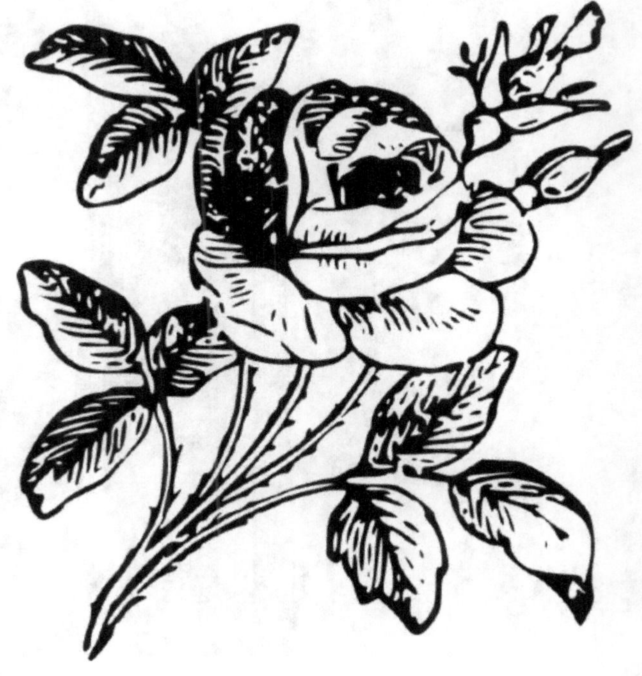

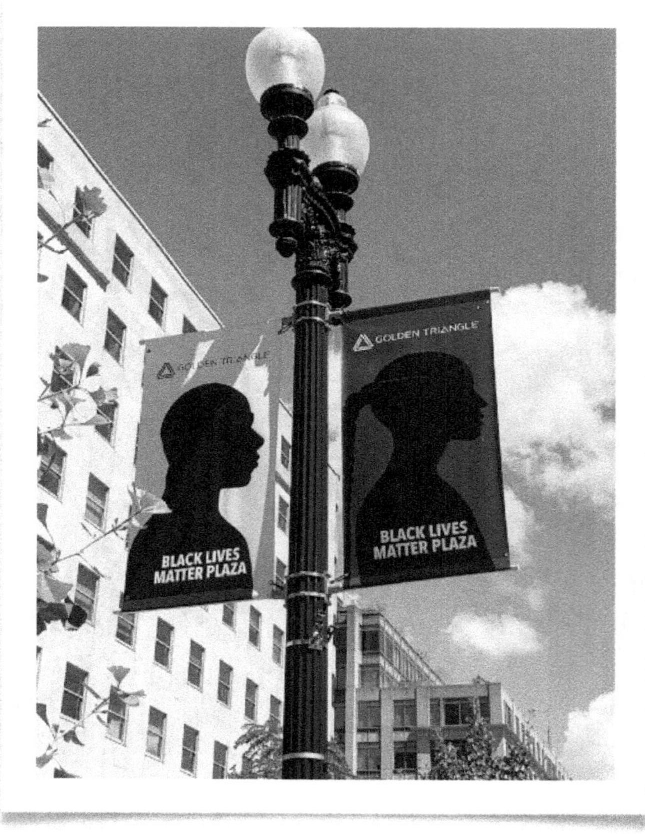
GOLDEN TRIANGLE
BLACK LIVES
MATTER PLAZA
GOLDEN TRIANGLE
BLACK LIVES
MATTER PLAZA

And Another One

Here we go again,
And tell me if you've heard this story before—
Another unarmed black man, killed, with the
murderers freely walking the streets months after the fact;
Sadly only coming to light because of a public
outrage that took 74 days to even gain traction;
Which honestly could have been the first of Nevuary
had the crime not been documented;
But even in the face of black and white, they create a
shade of grey to ensure their day in court;
To be governed by a judge, jury and defense that all
resemble them, and never the victim;
Rendering a verdict based on a system of laws
enacted for their benefit; and them only;
*This—my friend— is the f*ck sh*t we still protest;*
why to this day, we've never known true justice;
Because those authorized to carry weapons only feel
"threatened" in the presence of black people;
Regardless of age, sex or size;
But never when the offender is white.
This blatant hypocrisy is beyond infuriating—but
your suggestion is we should still pray for them as they prey on
us, right?
We should disregard their callous behavior towards

the minority and poor, and have faith that police
reform is speedily on the way… that's what you're saying??
Well, I call shenanigans, because lately, they've
seemed intently committed in spreading malevolence;
Almost daring to be charged or challenged in their
privilege, until the law goes against them;
Only then are we met with crying eyes and alibis
when their crimes are brought to trial;
And you know what, I'd be surprised too!
God forbid their rights are ever violated and freedoms
jeopardized— not in these United States!
But what do we do,
When the lawbreakers entrusted to enforce the law,
are protected by the lawmakers who pass them?
Therein lies the conundrum—
All I know is we need to seek real resolution, real
fast, before we lose another one,
And another one,
And another…

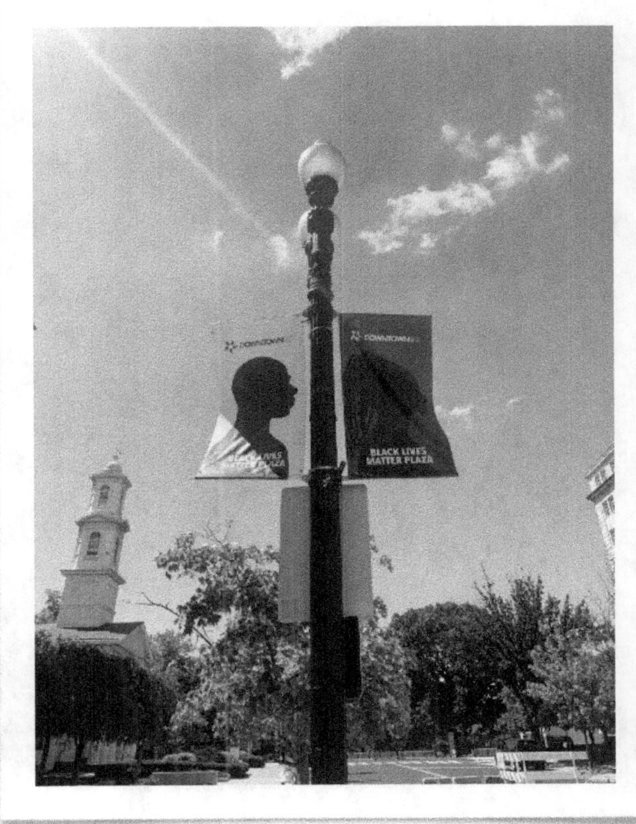
DOWNTOWN
DOWNTOWN
BLACK LIVES
MATTER PLAZA
BLACK LIVES
MATTER PLAZA

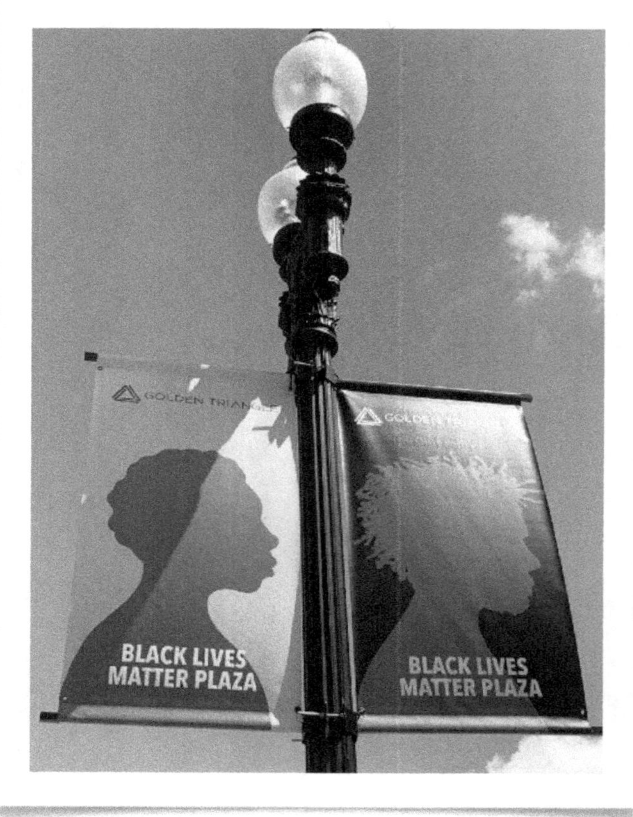
GOLDEN TRIANGLE
BLACK LIVES
MATTER PLAZA
GOLDEN TR
BLACK LIVES
MATTER PLAZA

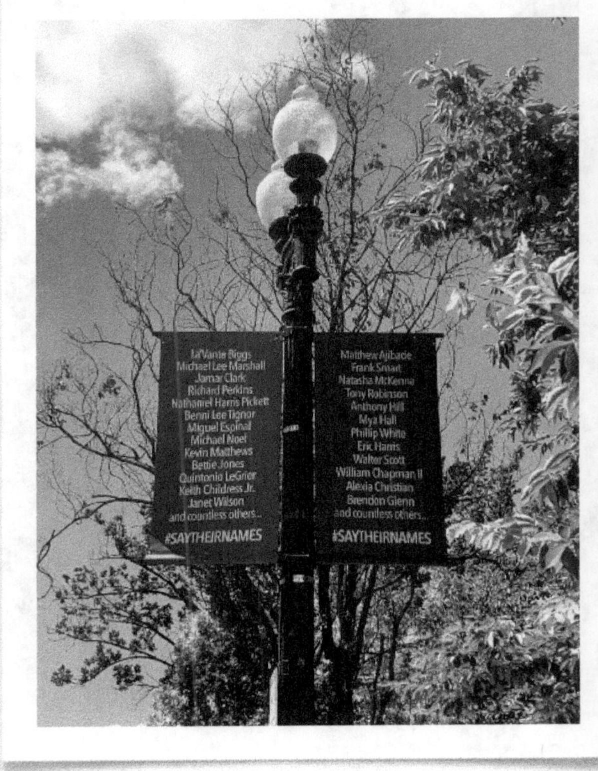
La'Vante Biggs
Michael Lee Marshall
Jamar Clark
Richard Perkins
Nathaniel Harris Pickett
Benni Lee Tignor
Miguel Espinal
Michael Noel
Kevin Matthews
Bettie Jones
Quintonio LeGrier
Keith Childress Jr.
Janet Wilson
and countless others...
#SAYTHEIRNAMES
Matthew Ajibade
Frank Smart
Natasha McKenna
Tony Robinson
Anthony Hill
Mya Hall
Phillip White
Eric Harris
Walter Scott
William Chapman II
Alexia Christian
Brendon Glenn
and countless others...
#SAYTHEIRNAMES

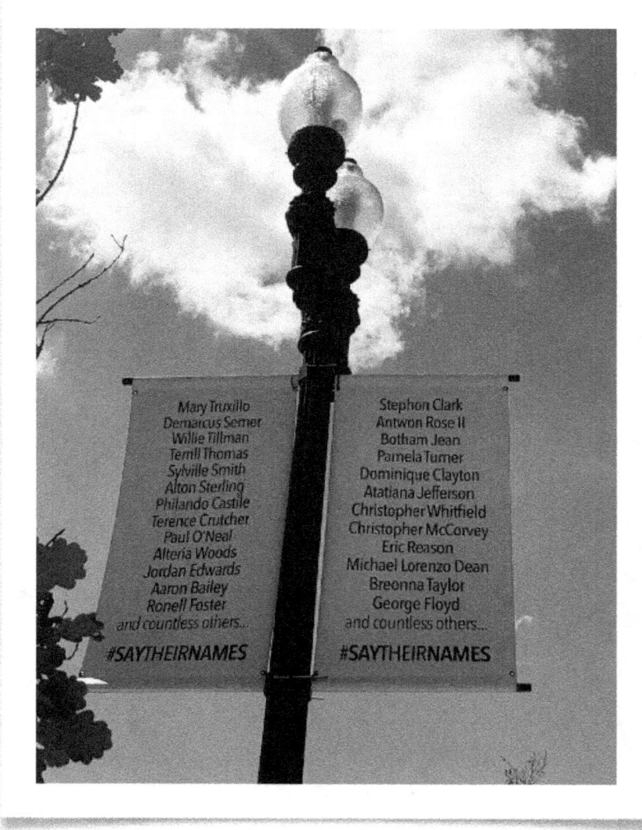
Mary Truxillo
Demarcus Semer
Willie Tillman
Terrill Thomas
Sylville Smith
Alton Sterling
Philando Castile
Terence Crutcher
Paul O'Neal
Alteria Woods
Jordan Edwards
Aaron Bailey
Ronell Foster
and countless others...
#SAYTHEIRNAMES

Stephon Clark
Antwon Rose II
Botham Jean
Pamela Turner
Dominique Clayton
Atatiana Jefferson
Christopher Whitfield
Christopher McCorvey
Eric Reason
Michael Lorenzo Dean
Breonna Taylor
George Floyd
and countless others...
#SAYTHEIRNAMES

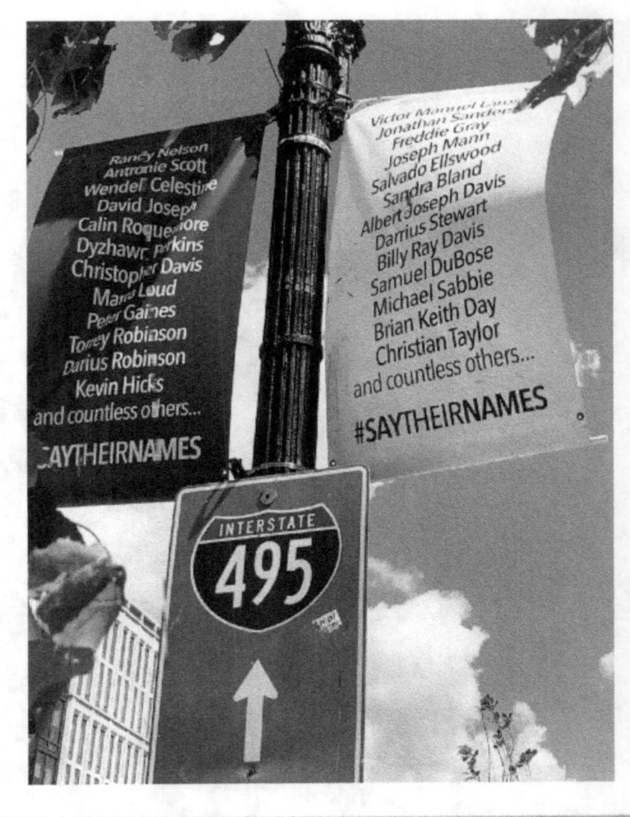
Randy Nelson
Antronie Scott
Wendell Celestine
David Joseph
Calin Roquemore
Dyzhawn Perkins
Christopher Davis
Marc Loud
Peter Gaines
Torrey Robinson
Darius Robinson
Kevin Hicks
and countless others...
SAYTHEIRNAMES
Victor Manuel Larosa
Jonathan Sanders
Freddie Gray
Joseph Mann
Salvado Ellswood
Sandra Bland
Albert Joseph Davis
Darrius Stewart
Billy Ray Davis
Samuel DuBose
Michael Sabbie
Brian Keith Day
Christian Taylor
and countless others...
#SAYTHEIRNAMES
INTERSTATE
495

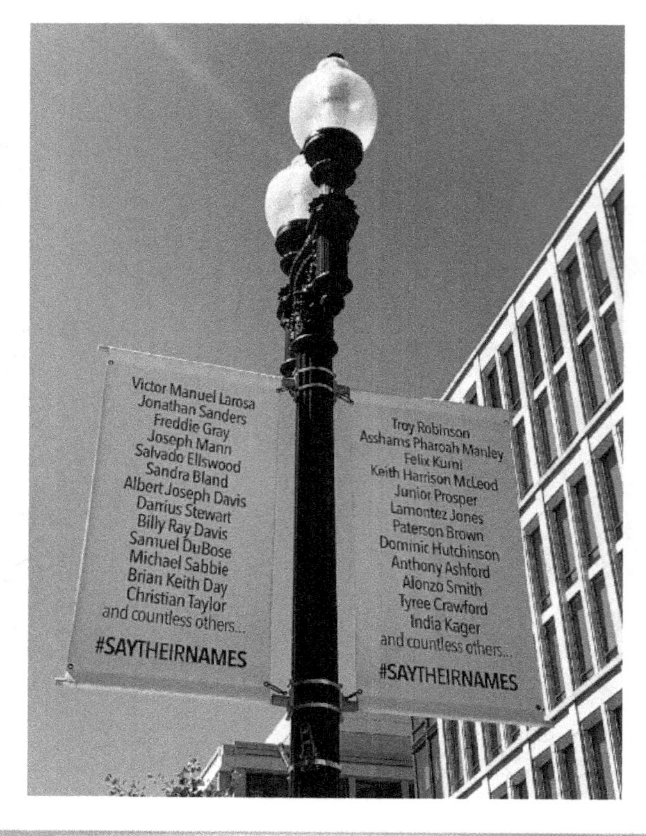
Victor Manuel Larosa
Jonathan Sanders
Freddie Gray
Joseph Mann
Salvado Ellswood
Sandra Bland
Albert Joseph Davis
Darrius Stewart
Billy Ray Davis
Samuel DuBose
Michael Sabbie
Brian Keith Day
Christian Taylor
and countless others...
#SAYTHEIRNAMES
Troy Robinson
Asshams Pharoah Manley
Felix Kumi
Keith Harrison McLeod
Junior Prosper
Lamontez Jones
Paterson Brown
Dominic Hutchinson
Anthony Ashford
Alonzo Smith
Tyree Crawford
India Kager
and countless others...
#SAYTHEIRNAMES

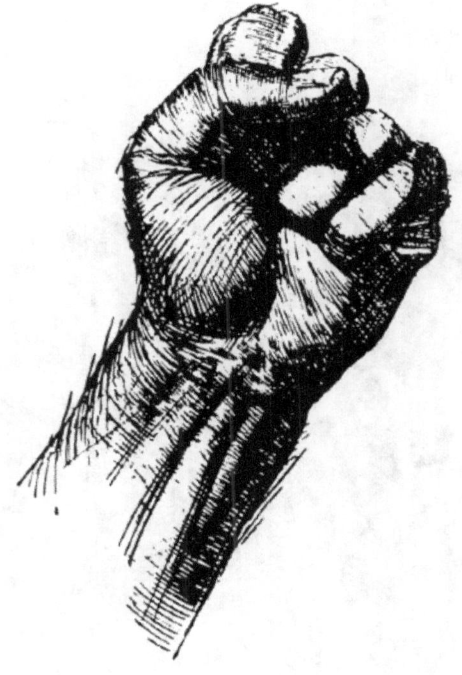

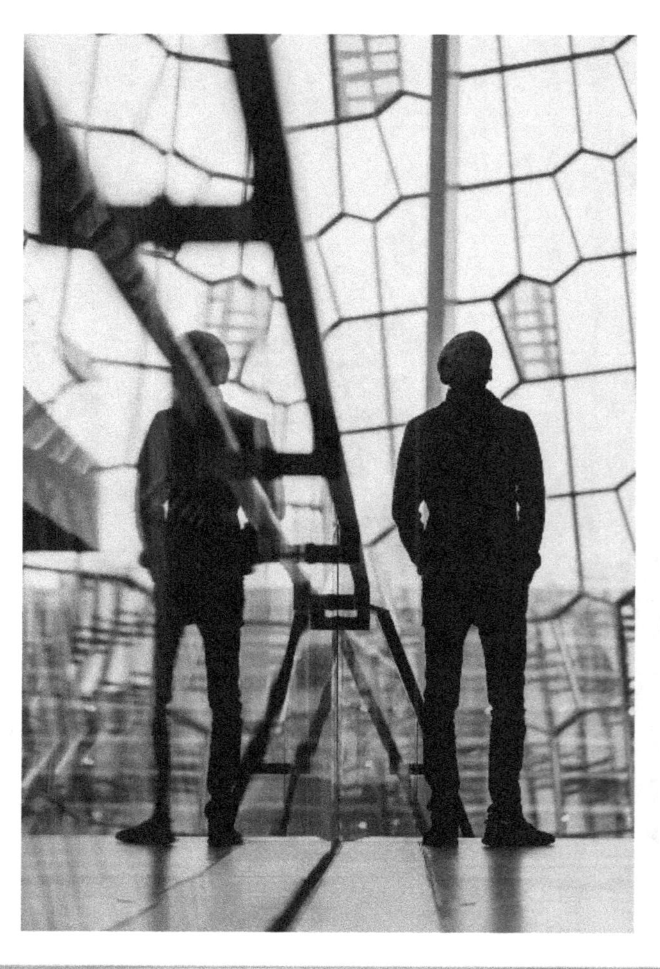

Mirror, Mirror

Imagine, for a moment, that we lived in a world
without them—
I suppose it wouldn't be much of a fairytale at all,
Given how the world is completely obsessed with how
well you adorn yourself;
For some, it would probably be torture—
Your perception constantly in question and your
appearance left to speculation, surely wouldn't inspire much
confidence;
What, then, would be our frame of reference but
another's opinion, without reflection?
Who would decide our standard of beauty, and
honestly, could you ever trust them?
If we were forced to rely on not what we perceive
with our eyes, but what our spirits intuit,
Maybe we'd feel more secure leading with our hearts;
Where the efficacy of your effort to win someone's
attention, would be dependent on the strength of an emotional
attraction instead of just the physical;
Would you be secure to reveal your truth though,
accepting the reality that your proposal may be rejected?
Perhaps…
Because whether we admit this or not, a fragility
exists with everyone's ego,
And sometimes, I know the mirror is there to mend

those broken pieces when it's been shattered;
Using the power of affirmation to rebuild that
security,
But I wonder if it were lost,
Your mirror,
What would you really have to offer?
Who are you, outside your projection?
Without your protection?

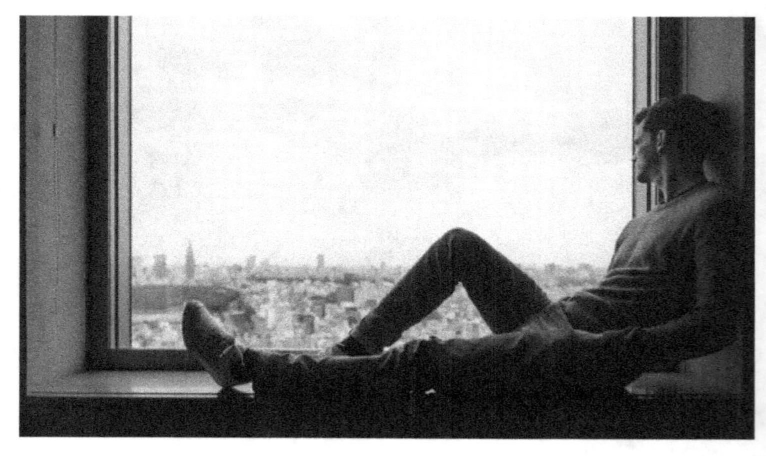

Wrong or Right?

I know I shouldn't say this,
But I believe I'm in a safe space, so I feel comfortable
to speak freely;
Full transparency—
Someone sent me a picture of me as a kid, and all it
did was bring back memories of being bullied by the
*neighborhood d*ckhead;*
Whose solo mission in life, it seemed, was to inflict
verbal and physical harm everyday including Sunday;
The reason my folks even enrolled me in martial arts
was solely because of him;
But from an early age, he had disdain for authority
and dared anyone to challenge him;
Unfortunately, I wasn't the only person on the
receiving end of his endless barrage;
But as distance and time put space between us, I
learned of his death returning home for a visit one day and
truly, I can honestly say, that I felt…nothing—
No pause for the fallen, not even an ounce of pity;
Which took a while for me to process because, for
some reason, I felt that I should?
Admittedly, I wanted him to feel the same pain he
caused others, but not by way of death;
Especially since he didn't even make it past quarter-
life;
So then,

Why did I feel a sense of relief when I heard the news?

That wasn't right, was it?

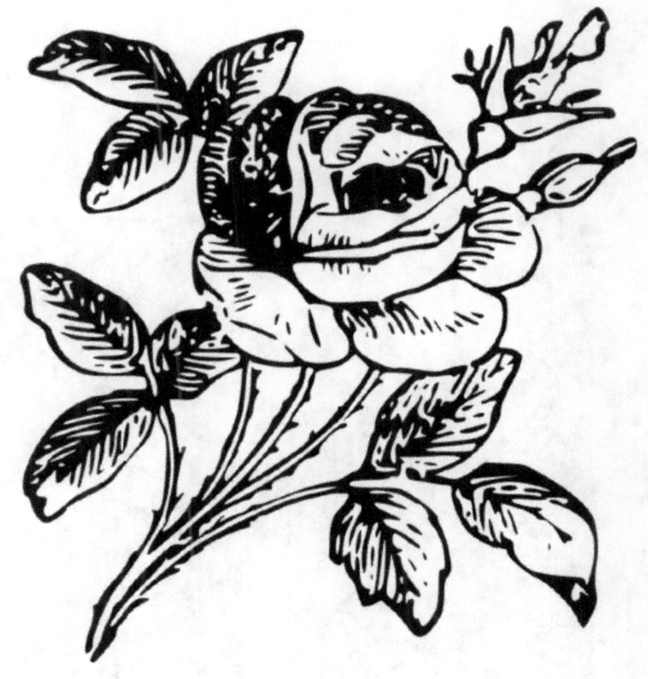

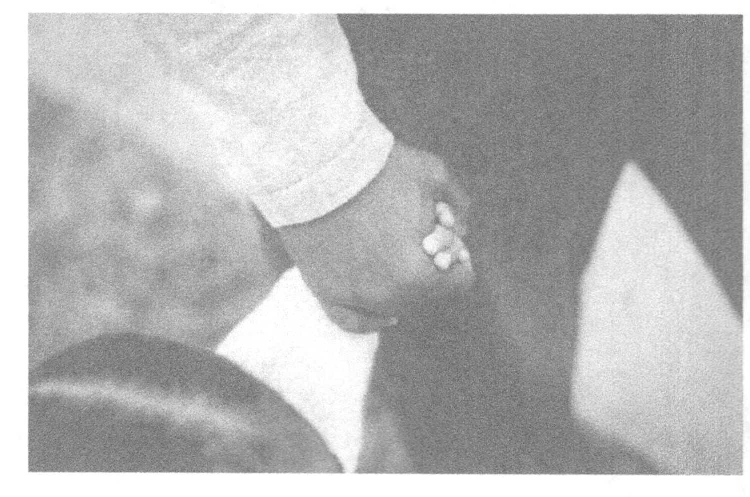

Next Up!

You ever wanted something so bad, but the fear of
failing kept you from trying?
Story of my life, right?
But in my next chapter, I genuinely want fatherhood
added to my list of occupations.
From my personal observation of friends and family,
I've been told it's a hell of a job—
But also the most rewarding according to them;
Even through sleepless nights, dirty diapers, incessant
crying and irritability; it's taxing they say,
But the general consensus is, it's worth every
deduction of energy expelled;
I just wasn't sold at the time;
Finances and living arrangements were always
inconsistent; with employment contingencies preventing
progression, I decided it was in my best interest to avoid
unnecessary responsibility;
Especially being the youngest of my generation, there
was really never a sense of urgency;
Most were already fulfilling their oath to be fruitful
and multiply, so my addition could wait;
But recent thoughts really make me wanna go half
on a baby,
Because I hate the idea of my bloodline ending with
me;
Granted I know the gift of having children is not

bestowed upon all,

And although the schematics aren't quite clear yet, at

least the doubt of my capability has been erased—

I can emphatically say, I'm ready to exercise my duty

and take my place in the order of procession;

And frankly, I'd be a dope dad!!!

I refuse to let all this swag and charming, good looks

the Lord gave me to go to waste!

Ok,

So it's settled!

Now all that's left to do is find the right one: If

you're interested in the vacancy, I'm currently accepting all

applications— serious candidates only!

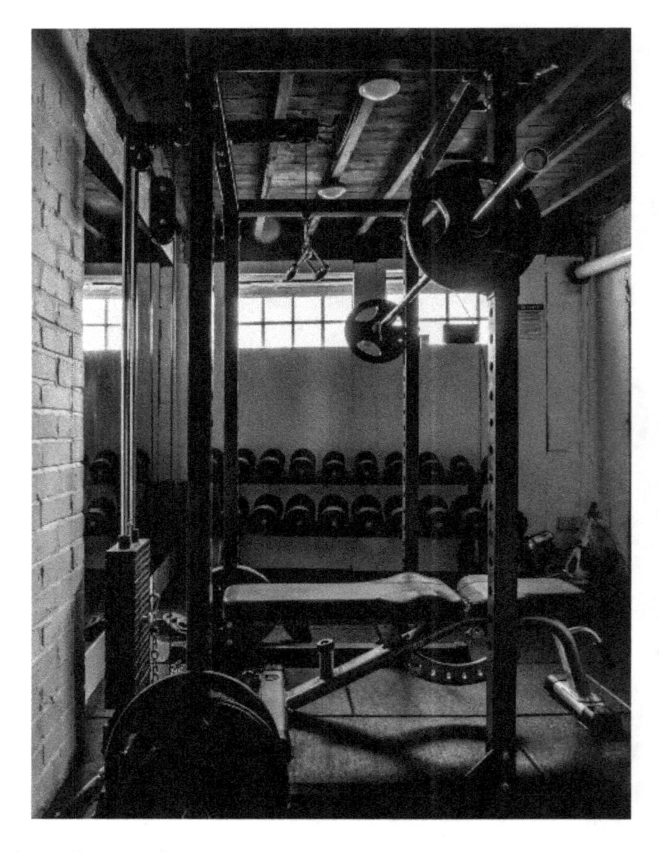

Full of it

I just can't with you—
The one thing you said you were gonna do,
Above all else if you ever had the time to commit,
STILL ain't been done after year, and I see no
motivation to even get started;
Still a procrastinator with all talk and no action I
see,
Because weights haven't been lifted, no stairs climbed
or miles ran; planks and push-ups you've avoided like the
plague;
*A sh*t diet with a healthy appetite for the wrong food*
has been a recipe for disaster, and you are solely to blame—
By now, there should have been some type of
definition, some piece of evidence that you've exercised care;
The lockdown is not a cop-out, especially when you
have gym equipment at the house, fully at your disposal;
So when it's time to hit the beach, don't be self-
conscious about being out of shape;
Sport that belly, wear it proudly and don't be
ashamed!
*Rick Ross that sh*t out, because you clearly aren't*
ready for the next level;
You're obviously content with your body image so

until you're actually serious,

Do me a favor,

And just shut the hell up!

88

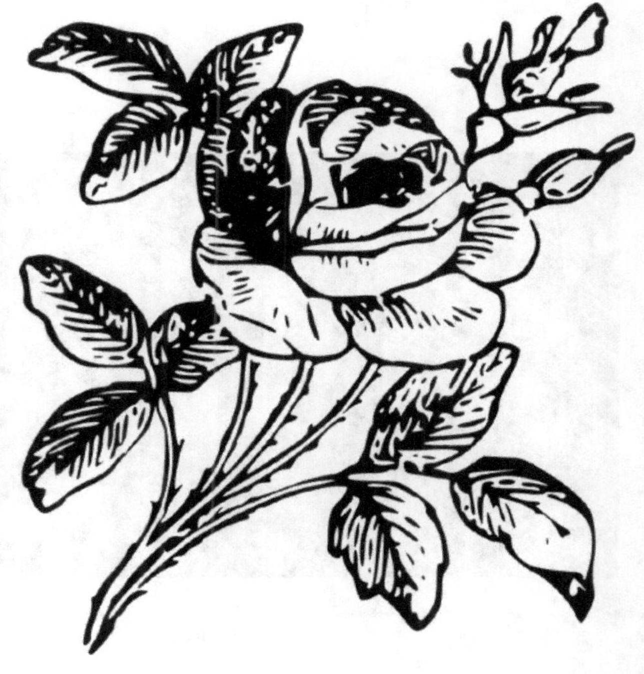

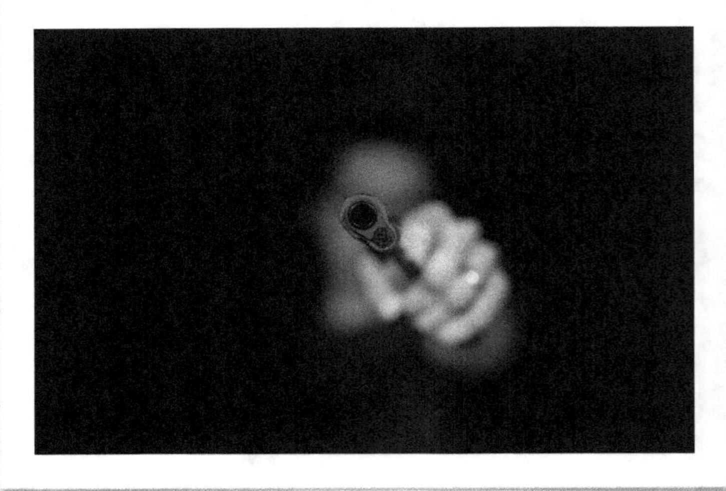

Strap Up

Well,
You heard it straight from the horse's mouth—
Gun violence is the new epidemic on our radar; 147
deaths last time I checked, is that correct?
And that's just from the start of '21 but it doesn't
seem like it'll stop; not when there's so much profit in
preserving the second amendment for Caucasians because,
Protection only pertains to the weapons inside of
*white hands; a permit doesn't mean sh*t for anyone else, even*
in a license to carry state—
We see what happens whenever blacks attempt to
liberate;
They get cast as militias and obliterated for daring to
bear arms against their intimidators;
Neighborhoods are infiltrated, establishments burned
and civilians killed in the most heinous ways;
Massacred as an example, to show our place in the
hierarchy of the racial divide;
Yet,
The most notorious and domestic terrorists we've seen
in our lifetime HAVE ALL BEEN WHITE!
From Parkland, Sante Fe, Sandy Hook and
Columbine;
To the Austin and Oklahoma City bombers, Las
Vegas and Charleston, South Carolina—

Gun safety has always been politicized as a partisan
issue where in fact, history proves it racial;
And no amount of background checks or reform will
settle the debt for the assault on our people,
Except by the blood of those who shed it—
And guess what?
It's time to collect!
This battle coming your way is not against man, but
against the one empowered to elevate and bring nations down
—and you don't stand a chance in hell!
Even with all your military might, your civilization
is on the brink of collapse;
War is inevitable,
And those same riffles used on us will now be used
for your own destruction…
Good luck!

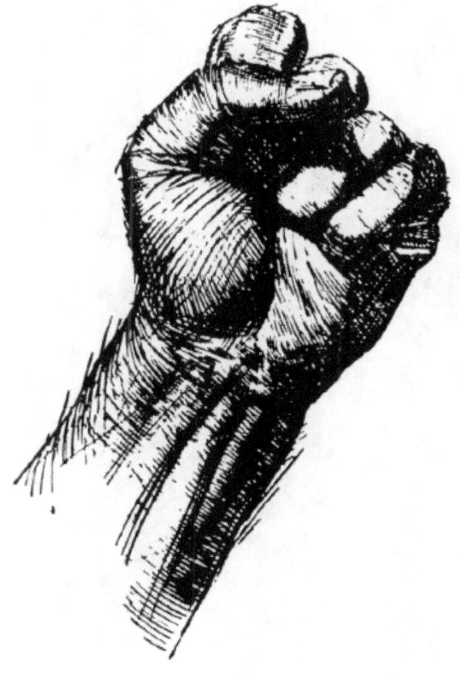

sweat is thinking about you
my heart pounds and i drip
drip
sweat is my anxiety
when i fail
when we fight
when i fumble
drip
      drip
sweat is when we intertwine
whose sweat is whose
drip
      drip
            drip
when i commute
when i dance
when i labour
i glisten
i let my work show

sweat

the lover

nadine bhabha

contents

the lover

the loveless

the city and everyone in it

the grind

the new

sweat

to my loved ones
thank you for the space, the love, the leg up, the
shoulders and the ears when i've needed them

to the inspirations
thank you for the perspective

Cover Art by Walt Ruston

Nadine Bhabha, author
Sweat / Nadine Bhabha

Edited by Suraya Bhabha,
and Safiyah Husein

Poems
Issued in print and electronic formats

ISBN- 978-1-7751991-0-6

sweat

POEMS BY

nadine bhabha

www.ingramcontent.com/pod-product-compliance
Lightning Source LLC
Chambersburg PA
CBHW051004060726
47593CB00017B/1027

i don't just care about you
i spend my days and nights thinking of ways to give
you all you need
how can i help [you] be happy?
how can i set [you] free?
i don't just love you
i don't just love anyone
i pour everything i have into all of you
my cup runneth over
and if i don't give you all my love
what is the point of living?

how come i forget your many faults when what i
need to do is get angry
you're perfect to me
when you're not perfect to you
snap the fuck out of it
brain's words falling on deaf ears
so i close my eyes and freefall back into a bed that
smells like skin and cookies and Pears and Dragon's
Blood and i wonder if you're eating burgers

he grabbed me and kissed me
i could really feel the missing
the longing
i haven't been touched in weeks he said
his body feels like home
having him was a dream
the nights felt full
the days felt round
he's the sugar
i'm the cream

bluenose
brown skin
black week
grey day
red night
pink lips
pink lips
cream skin
amber ale
white floors
purple sheets
brown eyes
brown eyes
the snow blinds me
and you are technicolour

-nights with [you], days without

i look at you and i think
no one can want to make you a snack more than i
do right now
or ever
let me always hold the key to your next donut
and love me forever

nadine bhabha

you were always licking salt from my skin
without complaint
i was the sea
when you were the coral
what a picturesque combination

your hands are the only things in this world that can
hold my emotions
you cup
you stroke
you cradle
your hands
they're rough like you have been working with them
all your life
mine are soft like i've never been outside
and that's where we argue
by the state of our hands
and i'm sorry

the time in High Park
behind the umbrella
dancing fingers
ants crawling beneath us
giggling and grumbling about not being alone
enough
a happy ending before rehearsal
you make me feel like we live life always driving at
a thousand kilometers an hour
i will never forget how alive i feel with you

that first day we spent in bed
was the most delicious day of my life
what a romance for the ages
we were patient
but so hungry
we played
we slept intertwined
we revealed truths
shed layers
shed pj's
i was on my side when your nose touched mine
it turned into a kiss
you wrapped yourself around me
and i waited to wake up
your mouth found my neck
if this was a dream i never wanted to wake up
to love someone for years and not even realize it
until they look at you like you hold the mysteries of
the universe in your eyes
is something i could never fathom happening to me
who me? no way. i would have said
that day my best friend became my entire world
nothing existed outside that bed
we didn't even eat
well
      i ate something
you nibbled on my soft and harder parts
i've never explored a body like that
i've never been so stimulated and relaxed all at once
heaven was real and it was in that room

i know you
are the sexiest words i have ever heard

-because you did

you asked
*do you want to hear what you want or what you
need?*
both?
*stop being a baby. stop whining. you will get
through anything*
but you know i'm here whenever you need me.
i'll take care of you

-you always knew how to clean up messes

i fall so deeply
i have to claw my way out

i counted the freckles and moles
memorized where and when and
when i was done
i knew you better
because your skin told me more than your mouth
ever did

to love someone a different colour is to put forth
into the world that you don't care who knows it. you
are making an unconscious statement to yourself,
your family, the entire population: that you love
freely. and we are all made from the same dust.

when we touched in a way that wasn't our normal
tickle
i felt superhuman
and delicate
more elegant than velvet

nadine bhabha

in the dark
your breath on my neck
made life worth living a thousand times over

your bed wasn't just a mattress on slats of wood
it was my shelter
my therapist's office
my massage parlour
my kitchen table

nadine bhabha

when i set my sights on you
i knew
if you licked me
my body would turn into a hurricane
and i would soak the whole world
with the delectable violence of my lust

sweat

you're a cigarette i want to hold between my lips
i want to drag
you til you're ash
i don't even smoke but i could fill my lungs with
you
let me get you between my lips

nadine bhabha

a relationship is a garden
it needs work
it takes time
it requires patience
an abundance of shit can help it thrive
when it's in bloom
it's a sight to behold

i remember the exact minute i fell in love with you
we had gone to ink my ribs
an elephant named bowie
we were on the bus
you know that's love
anyone who can feel love on the ttc should be given
a medal
we stared at each other for a second
i saw everything i had ever wanted and everything i
could ever want in your eyes
i thought
i could be deeply content with this man
i wanted to kiss you
but
you closed your eyes to rest
and the feeling did not go away
i was not being hypnotized
in that moment
i felt like i could take on any shape
i was spellbound

nadine bhabha

brush my hair with your words
draw crop circles on my spine
kiss warm milk into me
i'll rest here a while

-putting me to sleep

my eyes water
with how spicy your mind is

nadine bhabha

he holds me like
i'm the most delicate fabric
that he hungers to unravel

my tulips in the ocean
he laps up the salt
the tide rolls in where lightning strikes
he dares to fit the whole world in his mouth
i sit back and purr

nadine bhabha

this meeting of palms is a dozen roses
it's dinner already made
it's all my favourites illuminated by vanilla-scented
candles
these interlaced fingers are a surprise vacation to
anywhere beachy
the decadence of it
makes me want
makes me
        me

-holding hands

you came to me at a time where i looked at myself
and wondered why i wasn't
enough
i wondered why i was so easy to get over
you came to me at a time when all i wanted
was for you to see me like i saw you
but neither of us knew that until we
let ourselves sink
you made me believe that there can be a blur
between dreams and reality
night can turn into day
i realized that even though i sweat at the idea of not
knowing the next move
i was exhilarated by knowing it would be *us* who
would face the abyss

i love you
do you love me?
you said this to me tonight
i wanted to say it last night
first
but i got scared
so i kept my mouth shut and my legs open
i loved you last night too
and every night from there

sweat

the loveless

nadine bhabha

the loveless refers to
the empty space between us
the thing i am holding on to for dear life
even when you have let go
and never looked back

i am not blameless
i share culpability in my own heart break
i have ugliness about me that i am not proud to
admit
you tried.
i felt it
i still smell the trial and error on my skin
you didn't want to hold on to error
i will always feel that
yet there was so much more story for me
i was willing to be whatever you wanted
i didn't want to wear any other colour than your
favourite
that was the beginning of the end

i never decided to love you
i tiptoed into lust and fell off the cliff
into unadulterated love
i fell
and fell
until i hit bottom
the fall was spectacular
our could-be life flashed before my eyes
then i woke up

dear [you],
please stay out of my dreams
it's devastating to see you every night when you're
not even there
i can't touch you
my skin is cold with sweat
you haunt my days

-a different form of ghosting

i fear that i'm missing out
when you're the one
you're the one who won't know
what i can give
how good your life can be
but that is not comforting
it's hopeless

-you think you know what you're missing

sweat

my body is the best it will ever look
and there are no eyes to feast on it
no hands to devour it
no mouth to engulf it
no skin to graze at night
a waste of luscious terrain
i feel no desire to be desired by
anyone
       but you
i want to step inside my freezer and wait

i miss your night terrors
they made you less perfect
and i thanked god i didn't make you up
because i loved you for years
i can convince myself anything is real if i think
about it hard enough
but i wished for you and you came true
and those nocturnal interruptions made you feel real
to me.
i was there to say *it's ok, go to sleep.*
and then you weren't there
vanished into thin air
and i swear i made you up

you have to be whole without him
i know i've asked for help
i know i sought your advice
but it's so hard to take it when you've never been
broken
you've never been left
you've never given it all and been told you are not
enough
i appreciate the caring
but i'm still left searching for solace
i know i disappoint you all with my weakness
but i can't help it
i admit defeat

-letter to that friend

he sets my soul on fire
but i have no idea where i stand
will i ever be able to eat pancakes again without
thinking of him?
fat chance
he says coffee reminds him of me
there i am
immortalized in grinds
i hope he smells me every morning for the rest of
his life

text me instead of him
i have said this to many of you
how on earth could i minimize such big emotions
and unanswered questions and reduce it to *just send*
it to me instead
now that i am going through it
i feel like a world class asshole
because this is an impossible task
sure, i was your sponsor and now you are mine
but i want to punch you when you say to leave him
alone
how can you not indulge my heartache?
stop being such a good friend to me
i don't deserve it

i bought some incense today to calm my nerves
all it did was rile me up
it reminded me of lazy days
and Kangaroo
and those 3 hours
or was it 6
who are we kidding, it was 16 days straight
i'm going to live inside you
and you did
though you're gone
you never left

the worst thing of all
is lying to myself

nadine bhabha

the amount of minutes i spend looking out the
window
waiting
for the stranger you are to me now
to appear
and tell me it was all a mistake
you couldn't have said those things
you never meant them
you need me
it was me all along
i could string those minutes into a lifetime
two lifetimes
the ghosts of you and me

is it my destiny to find men who love me on a
clock?
is it coincidence?
rather than a deliberate decision
i get a *fancy seeing you here*
emotional baggage and i keep running into each
other
how do i sniff this out?
do i prevent?
do i sit along for the ride?
i wish i knew if i should go it alone

i ran into your friend in the lobby of where i work.
       cornered.
she reintroduced me to her fiancé
you remember nadine, [your] partner?
and i can't breathe
but i smile
yes, that's me
he remembers
oh. i didn't recognize you for a second
i think, *it's ok. i don't recognize me either*

anxiety is my only companion
and a mean one at that

you came
you saw
you conquered
you saw
you came
rolled over and fell asleep

empty hearted
full of mind
no sleep

nadine bhabha

you destroy me
just wreck me from the inside out
you know what you're doing
you know the radio silence wounds me
i need to hear your voice
but it hurts to hear it
are you helping or hurting by ignoring me?
i wish i was sane enough to know
you say you'll never forget
but the silence bubbles under my skin
it doesn't matter the reasons why we don't speak
all that matters is the single solitary fact
that i have not seen your face in months
and i feel like i've joined the ranks of the others
it doesn't matter that you said i'm different
i just feel like them
like when the world tells you you're special
and you know you're just like everybody else
i know i'm not special
because you thought i wasn't good enough to hold
on to

you left me at a time where i look in the mirror and
wonder why you didn't want to stay
why i wasn't enough
you left me at a time where i wondered why i am so
easy to get over
i see those pictures of you
smiles painted on your faces
arms wrapped around her
meanwhile i turn down any word of kindness
because i am turned off by the idea of anyone but
you
i know i pushed
i am hard to love, i know
you watched my first shattering heartbreak unfold
yet you still ignited the second one
(as if it was written in the footnotes of our love)
i am left wondering why i don't want me

how is it that time feels like distance?
the more hours pass the farther away you become
how do you smell?
does your hair naturally fall to the left or right?
there are oceans between us we count in days
months are planets
before the months become years i'll
have surely left this earth
for there will be nowhere else to go

i never thought i was in the one of two kinds of
people
one kind lives with depression
and one does not
but when the darkness birthed from deep in my
bowels
it coiled itself around my lungs
the lack of oxygen to my brain made it painfully
clear;
depression, just like everything else in this world,
lives on a spectrum
mine was a sleeping dragon
your leaving woke it
it burned everything i knew to be good
it made me feel like queen of the ashes
there was no morning
i stewed in my sweat, and stupidity, and waited
bed beckoned at all hours
nothing made me smile
love was behind me now
there was no morning
i knew better than to let myself be clouded by the
dark
but i could see no light
like i said,
there was no morning

it's not that i don't know who i am without you
it's that i know exactly who i am
and i don't like it

let me the fuck in
fists pounding on the door
i'll kick this shit right down!
does a peephole work both ways?
if you don't let me in, i'll break in! don't test me!
and she did.
once inside they couldn't go back.
who wants to live in a home they've broken into?
breaking down your walls has left me
feeling like a goddamn criminal

nadine bhabha

if i turn you into a poem
then you are as i write you
you're as soft or coarse as i make it
you wind with my words
and in my verses
you leave the weapons at home

today was a bad day
can't stop shallow breaths
can't stop retreading over texts
familiar stomping grounds
trying to eat pad thai and concentrate on work
but i can't
my meditation app told me
i'm feeling too many emotions for one day
i'm being judged by a computer
all roads lead to you

he wants the cool girl
i was always cold, but never cool
i have too much fire in my belly to be cool
nonchalant is absent from my dna
he wants simple
easy
i have never been easy
not for him
not for anyone
not in any sense of the word
he wants his best bud back
but we were always about to be in love before we
finally pulled the trigger
i do not know what friend i was to him when my
heart waited
ticked on a timer
waiting to explode when one day he touched me
differently
that touch had poison
but we both drank it up like water
he filled me up with warm
he filled me up with hot
he filled
i drank
then it stopped.
how could he go from scorching to freezing me out
and expect me to just be cool?

you're my favourite book
if i pick you up to read you again
my heart will break for a countless time
you're a history i have to put away
not a bible i can come back to

nadine bhabha

i miss you on rainy days
when we took refuge in sheets
and watched Eleven try to find the upside down

follow your dreams
if i followed my dreams
i'd be arriving on a stool
across from you at your bar
looking as perfect as the day you left
i would wrap our memories around your mind
let you come back as if nothing happened
you'd tell me it was all a dream
and i'd make this our new reality

nadine bhabha

when i think of your feet
how hairy and kind of ugly they are
i laugh
because if i saw your feet with my feet
(closed my eyes)
they were so soft
and warm
and the good kind of dry
and i miss them most of all
even when you grumbled at me for leaving
landmines of my crunchy disposable lenses
your feet were my playmates when the rest of us
slept

i have insane thoughts when i think about
what i would do if we stopped talking for good
we are over
but someone please tell my heart that
she still longs
we are over
but someone please tell my head that
she's filled with only good memories
we are over
but someone please tell my gut that
she churns with confusion,
and regret,
        and pain,
                and hope
am i crazy for wanting to present myself
at your door draped in all your favourite things?
she googles how to turn herself into a cinnamon bun
maybe then he'll invite me in

nadine bhabha

hot boys
and cold beer
will ruin you

i miss you on sunny days
when we'd find a patio
and drink coronas upside down
in margaritas and laugh about my armpits

not ready to see me
you know i'd wear that dress
no bra
that smile
no shame
those pinks and reds you like to see against my skin
you know i'd treat your body like a rock climbing
wall
exploring each curve and dip
taking us both to the top
that's why you're not ready to see me
you're afraid i'll make you forget why we stopped

my mind is gripping
what my hands have long let go

who says we can't find each other again
in the middle of the maze of ifs and whens
my nose is keen
and baby you are in the air tonight

sweat

you said you would teach me how to
skin,
gut,
and eat
a fish
we just didn't know we'd practice on me

nadine bhabha

i miss you on cold days
when it felt like the city was turned upside down
and
we lived inside a snow globe
but we drank so much hot coffee
i wasn't chilled to the bone

sweat

i can't even begin to think of your lips on someone
else
the shape of them brings me to my knees
the roughness of your cheek makes my heart beat
like a hummingbird at warp speed
please do not rub your cheek on another woman's
face
your cheek belongs to me

-scared to fall out of love

the last 48 hours can be counted in tears
honestly i'm surprised my bedroom didn't flood
and then engulf me
i have a beautiful dress that would just flow
and i have a number of hair garlands to choose from
and then they would say *how cliché, she actually
pulled an Ophelia*
and it would be true
because, my dear, you drove me mad

the mints in my coat pocket are a little
fuck you
from my former life when i was happy
and our kisses were winter green

lord knows how i didn't get in my car and drive to
you today
or last night
or the night before
or the night before that
or any of the nights from the past month
a divine hand squeezes my shoulder and says *no*
or maybe it's my friends' voices in my ear
or maybe it's my will power (for once)
or maybe it's the fact that i no longer know your
work schedule and i don't want to face your
roommates alone
because [our mutual friend] has seen my heartbreak
before
it's probably the deep desire to not look pathetic that
keeps my feet rooted to the floor
or couch (if i'm being totally honest)
either way
you're welcome
because i would have shown up and destroyed both
of us

sweat

feel/think
want/need
brain/heart

-at odds

you were the beginning and middle
this can't be our ending

i miss you on windy days
when the umbrella was blown inside out
and flipped upside down
and our hair made us look like a lion and a chia pet

i fear entering a room and not actually being alone
that someone is lurking
but then i get into bed
and i fear being alone
that no one is waiting up

-a house to myself

my hands go empty without your weathered grip
he said
*i don't like holding hands, but i know you like it, so i
do it*

when the rest of my life is good
but it's in the background
you are miraculously clear and standing in front of
me
but you want to be blurred
you want to disappear
i keep painting you richer and richer

-fading

sweat

waiting
…
…
…
is the hardest game of skill out there

the desire to feel nothing is the world's cruelest
oxymoron

i'm too nostalgic for my own good
everything i own that you've ever touched
i need it to touch me back
your shirts are losing your smell
i've hidden a pair of your boxers in my drawer
i can't stop staring at us smiling back at me

you're still the only person i can share a bed with
no one else feels right
or comfortable
now i sleep next to your dent

the only weapon of mass destruction with any clout
is love
we all know it

i asked you about her
and you didn't use her name
thank you for that
but it still annihilated me
i threw up beef ribs and red wine
it looked like thick blood in the white porcelain
bowl
and then i wandered around my own city like a
stranger not understanding the people or the
buildings or what the chirp of the crosswalk meant
the day was gray
i felt deaf
foggy and hazy
i spoke no language
the only name i could remember was yours

sweat

the city and everyone in it

i am comprised of all the lights
sights
sounds
and voices i encounter
in all the moments i am awake
my city
my people
my strangers
there is comfort in these things

sweat

to my family:

mum; you're strong, simultaneously fragile
i vacillate between learning from your mistakes,
swerving certain traits,
and wanting to be exactly like you
you passed down your oceans of emotions
your temper
your face
your loyalty
your longing to be loved
your vocabulary
your warmth
your hands and all the food they make

daddy; you knew everything
and when i realized you were
still figuring it out i couldn't compute
i got your hard head
your temper
your rock 'n' roll
your strength
your quiet understanding
your sense of play
your sense of direction
your longing to be wanted
your ability to fix

without them i would be
a poor excuse for a human being

they taught me that love takes many forms. it's not what we see in the movies. it's not what your grandparents tell you is right. the answers don't even lie in self-help books or art. it is unique to two people. and it can change. you have to be able to adapt with that person or you don't. happiness can live in two houses. happiness can include space. happiness can have self-exploration both alongside and aside from another person. the invisible line can stay tethered in distance. they taught me trial and error, how to make a house a home, and how to fight back with both fists at the ready.

-not your typical marriage

sweat

my brother has taught me
the bottomless power
of an open mind

-a sequoia among a family of rivers and stones

you are every blossoming flower. a purple symbol of life. though younger, i've learned more from you than anyone else. in a past life we were twins. in this one, impatience is my middle name and i ran out of the womb two years ahead. i pity those who try to hold a candle, for you're an entire chandelier. you know the why and how and if you didn't, you could make it up and i would believe you. a call out to sisters everywhere to know yours. to know mine is my greatest accomplishment.

sweat

the construction is so loud
i can't hear my own road rage

-toronto pt 1

nadine bhabha

hell hath no fury
as a commuter
in negative twenty degrees
waiting for a bus
that is not in service

-toronto pt 2

my city sounds like
3 subway chimes.
it's people saying *sorry* in endless languages.
a man thumping a bible bursting with *believe in the
lord* across from the men coaxing you to islam.
it's someone asking you for cans in the park.
it's the lake rushing towards and away from the
ferry.
it's muffled music outside of every door down King
street on a saturday night
and the subsequent sound of a horse clip-clopping
while on duty.
it's children screaming at a splash pad.
it's my name being called from across a busy
intersection.

-toronto pt 3

nadine bhabha

riding the rocket
the dull murmur of the rails
and the commuters
and the rush
and above it all
a woman without a destination sings loudly;
set me free so i may love again!
and like that,
i get to where i'm going

-toronto pt 4

sweat

dundas street on a tuesday
an ordinary day
as i debate between the bank or the library first
a man stops me
instead of leering
instead of asking for change
instead of making my dress feel sheer
he says *don't let love destroy you*
and i crumble all the way back home

-toronto pt 5

nadine bhabha

this city is rich
it has opened my mind
and taste buds
to tastes of the world
it taught me
love is love is love
i have shed tears in so many of its theatres
shared laughs on many of its patios
felt love for my neighbours on many of its streets
from lake to sky
i will always feel tied to this home

-love letter to toronto

wishing i could see into the future
so i could have known
you were just passing through
you taught me about time
how fast it moves
and to hug the people i love
i wish we knew to slow it down
in those days
i want to know what you think of who rihanna has
become
since we listened to pon de replay
in your mitsubishi lancer
remember when we burned cds?
you're alive to me on discs
you are the earth and wind
i remember every july and september
to give an extra hug to those i love

-geetesh singh 1988-2009

nadine bhabha

i hunger for a life
that satiates
for a love that is not precarious
for a future i can grab
hold in my hand
lasso around bigger dreams
my mouth is wide open
so feed me, city
feed me all night long

sweat

the grind

are you there beyoncé?
it's me,
nadine…

i don't want what you want
for me.
because i am a dreamer
and you never sleep

-don't try to discourage what can't be persuaded

i'm the only chocolate chip
in this cookie

-the industry

my guts twirl like a tornado when i know my art is
working
not on them
but on me

nadine bhabha

want to make love,
or do you want to make art?
it's all the same to me

sweat

sometimes i know i am bullshit
i am drivel
i am my work
my work is always in a state of flux

-imposter syndrome

you don't need to tell me that artists usually fail
if anyone knows that, it's me
and how dare you
how dare you see tiny pay checks and equate that to
failure?
how dare you see followers and equate that to
success?
no one needs to tell me how my industry works
i bleed this life every day
and you sit there (my god that's a high horse) and
tell me i might fail
yes
i might
i kind of want to
because i'll live to tell the tale
and that will fuel my art

-cycle

sitting in a room with a dozen stunning brown faces
i wish we could all get it
but i hope i am chosen
this is the thin line between community and
competition

-the audition room

i was a frizzy little thing
i did not know how to wear my hair
my skin
my shape
other than my family
where could i find out
how i was supposed to look
tv did not tell me
magazines did not show me
no actor on stage could help me
i searched for examples in bodies that were
continents away from what i was living in
i stood out like a smudge on cream sheets
trying to blend brown into white

- popular culture for whom?

that letter i finally mailed
making a meal from
whatever
        is left
           in the fridge
a half written play
throwing out old receipts
getting through another night at the joe job because
i am an artist
and no one can live
        on determination alone
(determination does not pay for americanos)
sleeping through the night
breathing new life into an old shirt
walking along the lake
taking away from my last audition the fact that i
said my name and height with such a
      stunning confidence
i didn't know i had in me
laughing
starting and stopping and reconsidering this half
written play
perhaps it's now a web series
or a novel
calling my grandparents
making someone belly laugh
listening to my heart beating and reminding myself
that life
    is not
      a mountain
i am meant to be climbing

nadine bhabha

it is an ocean i can ride
and i am doing ok

- accomplishments in all their forms

crave
hit
crave
hit
all those fuzzy chemicals fizzing up my brain
making me foam at the mouth
drooling, begging
wanting more
it's never enough
i never want to come down
i'm addicted to the art in me

-work junkie

it's when i should feel my most confident
almighty
because i made it here
that's when
that's when a little voice
that ebbs and flows like the ocean in my ear
tells me i'm not supposed to be here
they might realize they've made a mistake
i stand on stolen ground
they didn't mean to pick me
and i'll be uncovered
it whispers *i'm not worthy*
every time i mine gold
i am afraid of being robbed of it
on account of my not deserving it
because deserve is a word that feels
intangible and watery
so i cower
and wait
hold my breath
and hope they don't find me out

-if a person succeeds and they can't enjoy it, does it
even count?

though they say it's the red in your blood and the
white on your teeth
the job goes to the creamiest
put the call out for the rainbow
but the space between ebony and ivory is no-man's
land

-yes, brown is beautiful, but can it sell?

when i learned that success
is not a pie
where my slice is not enhanced by the diminishing
of yours
only then did i understand
why i never felt full

-more than enough to go around

i'm an actor
i walk out into the black
every night
feel the heat of the unknown
even on a wednesday afternoon
i always walk out into the black

-i am not scared of the dark

just because i question a system;
a machine that keeps going unless someone
or many ones
throw a wrench in it
does not mean i question your legitimacy in this
world
i'm just asking you to help validate others
no one is saying your life is easy
i'm just saying
we can help make others' less hard

- race wars

you must have chameleon skin
and a lion heart
thick skin
sharp teeth
devour the rejection like snacks
hunger
hunt
feast
adapt

-artist survival skills

i'm moving at the speed of a tuesday afternoon
but i want my life to feel like an early friday
evening
with the whole night ahead of me and
i'm lingering in sundown

-hurry up and make my mark

i get these ideas in my head
dreams
fantasies
i don't have the part of the brain that says these are
just figments of my imagination
just my creative mind at work
because of this
i get lost in fantasy
disappointed when reality creeps in
i am always dreaming
living a parallel life
believing in another world
that is just ever so slightly out of reach

the industry roadblocks did not start at home
i was born into
no judgement
no one telling me i could not
or worse
should not
my parents knew only to nurture
encourage
how many parents of colour help their children be
artists
how many parents of women emphasize
strong-mindedness
leadership
ferocity
independence
yes even without a partner they told me i am whole
my siblings are gifts who learned about my world
have helped me run lines
while my parents make every dream as close to
realization as they can manage
not coming from art themselves
everything i crave
is made possible by
the foundation from whence i came

adulthood is one endless saga
of whack-a-mole
why don't they make mallets that hit them all?
i feel like i don't even own the right mallet
so i use my fists
and at first it's fun
at first i commend myself for dealing with mole
after mole, challenge after challenge
but it gets harder
i lose control of my limbs
i look over and someone plays better
hits harder
it doesn't look easy when they do it though
the game is rigged for all of us

- perspective

am i the only one overwhelmed by art?
a mural so vast
a sculpture so fine
a colour so bright
so rich
my heart aches
i feel small
small but full
i covet
i want to scream
i fall in love

sweat

the new

and then the sun peaks it's golden head out and
suddenly i'm fine
the future smells like grass
the pain is still close but i have to reach for it
like it's in my purse
to get to it i have to pass receipts from brunch,
theatre stubs,
a polaroid of my mum and i on friday,
half the granola bar i shared with my best friend on
a stoop on Queen street
and like that
i realize
i have everything

his touch is a bandaid, not stitches
resist the 3am urges
that's what they invented porn for
or whatever you're into
but there will be so many more hands
or just the right pair
now use those fingers for something more satisfying
than dialing his number

nadine bhabha

people are too complicated to put into two kinds
don't make the mistake of thinking
boys are bad or good
you know you have a sharpness to you
even though you're softer than cashmere
most nights
don't blame the boy
blame chemicals

he could not hold you
the cosmos inside you are too vast
you dream too big
you jump too high
you radiate too bright
he was afraid of you
he still is
so he stays away
kicking a can down the street
but you
you are a lake
an ocean
a galaxy of beauty
too deep to swim

nadine bhabha

you are more
not the bare minimum
not the essentials
not something to tide him over
to help him survive temporarily
you are all

-love letter to myself

sweet nothings are what to look out for with the
next one.
i'm afraid i'll hear real love come out and mistake it
for lust
or run away from it
because i can't bear any more kind words
that expire when i need them most

-give me donuts, not words

one day you'll be at work
or at a coffee shop
or doing something random
and completely unexpectedly
the energy shifts
you notice someone who is worth your eye time
the universe makes them notice you too
if you're at work, you get to know them
you ask the whos about who's that and the wheres
about what's the deals
and this small act shifts the energy again
if you're at a coffee shop or somewhere random
you're accelerated by the possibility of this being
the one and only moment so a fuck up is a moot
point
then in one moment of pure confidence that even
you don't know where it came from
you walk over and make a joke
he smiles
he makes a worse one
you smile twice
the smile turns into conversation
minutes turn into longer texts
and finally the offer of drinks or coffee or
something random is put out there
you'll go, get dressed up, get scared, excited,
anxious, sad, and energized in the hour it takes to
get ready and commute
the talking is easy
the looks are deliberate and lingering
and that night

and the next few nights
are spent talking on the phone
texting
giggling
no you hang up
date two turns into three
a week later
you still feel the same, but less sad, more energized
a month goes by
dinners at home fill the space where movies out
once did
he knows your whos
you know the whats and his deals
months are long and short
then one day it hits you
you're in love.
be open
be open to the possibility of the energy shift
that is where the magic waits

-dear self, again and again

women will always have my back
even when i have no spine
even when i feel like i will fall
and there's no safety net
they will stand behind me
as lovers
as thinkers
they will validate
they will commiserate
they will add colour to the ever-changing mural of
the female voice
and i will add mine
once i'm whole enough to find it

we all heal differently
alanis for the scorned
adele for the broken
rihanna or gaga for the badass bitch moving the
fuck on
and if you cannot choose, or fall into none of the
above
beyoncé
beyoncé
beyoncé
she will help you find your inner queen

i may look like i have thorns on my skin
i may speak sharply like my tongue is a snake
i may walk like i'm leading a pack
but my insides are soft and aching for someone to
caress them
i'm tired
so i search for someone to rest in

there isn't always a "because"
often just a dangling "why"

they see an artist
and fall for the magic in me
even other creative types
fawn over my fireworks
but when the light goes out
and my duality shows
(there is no light without darkness)
they cannot run away fast enough
they feel betrayed by my fire
when i am the one
who mistook infatuation for love

emotions change
they are moving organisms
why say *this is the way i am*
this is what i want
when we know tomorrow could make you believe
what you thought today was utterly ludicrous
become water
take shape as you encounter it
but flow when the container breaks

-malleability

nadine bhabha

it has taken me this long
to realize
that water is stronger than fire
and earthquakes
to be soft
is
to
overcome

-flies and honey and all that jazz

we need men
and men need us
and men need men
and we need sisters
because people need love
it's a simple as that

-my feminism does not oppress you

nadine bhabha

falling apart does not make me weak
and if it does
why is being weak an insult?
context my dears, context
allow people to see you fall apart
that is just one of the colours you possess
it is most tough to be soft

i feel like
i am made
entirely of
painted steel

i am a tree
i only thrive when my branches and roots are
healthy and thriving

-yoga and meditation go a long way

i just want someone to share a burrito bowl with me
kiss my forehead at the movies
and rub my stomach when i have cramps

nadine bhabha

i am a dormant dragon
my spine has hardened
one day
when the time comes
i will burn entire cities to the ground
on my way through the stratosphere
because the fire in my belly
is the only thing that keeps me warm at night

i got caught
and so did they
and so will she
i thought i'd always be a butterfly in your net
turns out i don't just flutter by
i am the field in which you frolic
and i deserve the sky

this new boy
kissed me like he knew me from the first touch
on my forehead
the back of my neck
the space between
i lay in the dark with a stranger
it felt so familiar
the next breath was full of relief
knowing i'll be a-o-fucking-k

we giggled like teens
stumbled to my room
my bed
i looked over to the unused side of it
the side i didn't want to sleep on
but with this new one (both of us full of wine and
tequila and music) i could barely remember why.
the sheets moved under me
as his sweat slicked his back
this mingling of saltwater
took me there
to the place where i forgot your name
for good

i have the kind of spirit that scares them away
be afraid, be very afraid
i am a giant in a land of tiny flowers
and only an everest can get in on this
only a mountain will move me

let me stroke that ego
til you can't stand it
then take a cold shower
now let our minds meet

-getting to know a new one

nadine bhabha

when the new one learns my coffee preferences
i may just propose right then and there

in the end
i don't want
what doesn't want me
it happened before
it happened again
now i must stop it from taking over my soul for a
third time
i will not love the loveless
i will not love the loveless
i will not love the loveless

nadine bhabha

the thing to know when taking care of oneself
is
it is ok to take
when you have nothing left to give

i have the type of sharp mouth
that allows people to think i'm unbreakable
it's a common misconception that words trickle
down me
leaving no impression
but sometimes they seep in
those words grow inside my bones
turn into forests
that penetrate my foundation
ivy words, termite words
even the strongest wall can crack
and i am far from the strongest

i can't help but think i have not lost you
just misplaced you
maybe i'll find you again eventually

the world is too wide
to dwell on empty love
open up to your tiny self
you will be a supernova

nadine bhabha

i had the moment
when my long-time friend came to visit on a
layover
and poured her heart into my palm
i had the moment
i realized
i just want you to be happy
i want me to be happy
whether we're now parallel or will one day again be
intersected
no one will ever be able to know for sure
except the twisted, sadistic,
magnificent
hands of fate

i am whole-heartedly excited
for the moment
one of us calls
and we talk like we used to
a joke is just a joke
we laugh because it's funny
not from nerves
not from courtesy
because we are both intact

you have more to give
and he knows it
you'll be happy again
and he shows it
a second or third chance—
you'd blow it
so now you must move on

fighting that feeling cause
he knows he needs you
wants to keep you, hold you,
but he knows he must free you
so now you must move on

and when you've wiped the tears from your eyes
and the shit from your heart, you'll see clear enough
to know there's a story ahead. a new one. not better
or worse, but different. fresh. clean. the kind of
story where you feel pure joy for those who've hurt
you because grudges are so last year. the only thing
between you and your old life is time. nothing has
changed. hope had mummified your emotions for
this so-called love of your life and time has now
eroded all preservatives. what's left is an empty
body. ready to be filled up with good food, (you
know cheese always has your back), friendships,
and all the rooftop patios that come with close talks
after midnight, and self-love; the best kind. the kind
that would never even entertain *do i look good in
this?* because you know you do. the kind of self-
love that is easily poured from head to toe and

oozes from your every pore every day in every way,
so you must keep filling and filling. this is where
you go now. this is what you do. you move on.

i never thought i was a poet
until words
like
      sweat
poured out of me
and suddenly
there i was

about the author

nadine bhabha is a toronto-based actor and writer.
this is her first collection of poetry and first time
sharing her writing with all of you. her poems have
themes of love, loss, heartbreak, growing up,
womanhood, trying to make it in the best industry in
the world, living in the greatest city in the world,
and finding self-love. she wants to thank you for
making it this far, and even if you just read one
page and it's this one, thank you.